HEALTHY EMOTIONS

HELPING
CHILDREN
GROW

HEALTHY
EMOTIONS

Mary Vander Goot

BAKER BOOK HOUSE

Grand Rapids, Michigan 49516

#743944

Contents

83p.

stop@60

Acknowledgments

Once a book is written it is almost impossible to adequately credit those persons who have in one way or another added their energy to the task. The difficulty is not due to the fading of memory but to the quantity and diversity of those contributions. There are five sources of support and encouragement which have been especially helpful to me in writing this book.

The background research was done in preparation for a course on emotion that I taught at Calvin College. My students understood that I needed a forum in which to present my initial ideas. They brought new ideas to life, demolished a few weak ones, and helped to polish some which were first presented to them in very rough form. They had the courage to respond to me out of their life experiences. I consider their contribution a very generous gift.

The writing of this book was sponsored by Christian Schools International with funding from the Christian Schools International Foundation and the Canadian Christian Education Foundation. My thanks to them for their support. Of special help to me was Joy Witte whose good humor and keen suggestions were a great encouragement.

My counseling associates, Peter Everts, Hap Frizzell, Bill

Van Dyke, and Tom Wilkinson have shared with me an environment in which real people work hard to heal emotions and enjoy new health in relationships. I muse on the earnest work of parents, children, and counselors with fond memories. I sincerely hope that this book adequately expresses my respect for their efforts.

Finally, my mother's emotional strength and tenderness were the context in which my own emotions first took their form; to her I am most deeply grateful. It was she who modeled for me that rich legacy of emotional life of which women have so long been guardians, but whose energy and richness is really meant for us all. To her I dedicate this book.

Mary Vander Goot
Grand Rapids, Michigan
September 1986

Introduction

Not long ago I joined some friends to celebrate the birth of a new baby. This baby is a darling, the kind scouts for advertising companies must dream about. In addition to being beautiful this particular baby had the social grace to fall asleep right during the party. There she was on the floor, in the middle of her circle of visitors, framed by a brand-new, baby-soft blanket, deep in that exquisite, peaceful sleep that is God's special gift to babies.

The scene was captivating and her visitors kept making adoring comments. But the spell was finally broken by a fellow who muttered, with a touch of humor but also some seriousness, "Too bad life won't always be that easy."

I suppose it's true. My little friend will have to grow up. All of the admirers who gathered after her birth wouldn't wish it any other way. We can all wish that overall her life will be happy and pleasant, but we also know that it won't always and at every moment be so. Growing up will have its good and its bad times. Her parents will do what they can to give her emotional support. They are the kind of mom and dad who will encourage her to develop robust emotions for both good times and bad.

This is a book about emotions, about the normal emotions

of normal children. Its purpose is to help adults deal with children's emotions effectively. Emotional problems are not allowed to take center stage in the discussion, because this book works with the assumption that most feelings are healthy, and if they are sensitively understood they can be put to good use. That is not to overlook the fact that some emotions are unpleasant or threatening. Of course, some emotions are downright ugly. But even ugly emotions need to be worked out, unknotted, and turned back toward health.

Emotions are very cumbersome creatures if you try to catch them in a theory. Psychological researchers have developed good theories about lots of things, but the theories they have constructed about emotions have been some of the most difficult to understand and apply. That remains a problem for researchers, but it is not an insurmountable problem for the rest of us.

There is another way to learn about emotions. Because we all have emotions we can learn a great deal by reflecting on our own emotions. As we do that, we can begin to identify the variety of them, and those emotions we identify we can also name and describe in words. There is a ripple effect in our reflections. Emotions translated into words open up for us the possibility of sharing emotions with others, and emotional companionship is a very important ingredient in healthy adjustment.

Even though the focus of this book is helping children develop healthy emotions, thus far we have only mentioned that we can develop insights by learning to reflect on our own emotions. Actually, that is quite to the point. The most valuable asset adults have for helping children develop healthy emotions is the understanding adults have of their own emotions.

In singling out emotional development and identifying it as an important aspect of children's growth, we need not assume that it takes priority over the other aspects of their development. For example, it is equally important for children to learn appropriate social behavior at home, in school, and in the neighborhood. Similarly, the formation of conscience—ability to make sound moral judgments, and a sense of what is just and equitable—are important tasks of childhood. Emotional growth occurs alongside and is intertwined with these other features of development.

There are some special concerns that arise among Christian adults who address the matter of wholesome nurture, and it is the intention of the discussion that follows to be especially sensitive and respectful toward the commitments of Christians who wish to make faith relevant to daily life. At the same time, this book does not limit its concern to the well-being of Christian children only, but rather grows out of a genuine commitment to the well-being of all children, everywhere. It is this broad concern that is the context for our specific focus on emotion.

To help the adult reader of this book become oriented to thinking about emotions, the first two chapters are of a general nature. Chapter 1 considers what we discover when we reflect on our own emotions. It introduces terms and serves as a reminder of some of the subtle features of emotions that we notice when our attention is drawn to them by words. The next chapter introduces some goals of emotional health. It is easy to talk about good feelings, but what are some distinguishing marks of emotional health? That is what chapter 2 will explore.

In chapter 3 we begin to focus on children's emotions by examining the bridge between adults and children. How do children communicate their emotions to adults, and how do adults shape the emotions of children? In chapters 4 and 5 we look at some of the emotional tasks children need to complete during childhood.

As we examine emotional milestones, we notice that parents are not the only important adults in children's lives, so in chapter 6 we go on to look at the emotional resources that children can find in relationships with adults outside of the family. Then in chapter 7 we review some ways in which the emotional growth of children is shaped by their experiences at school.

Some readers may finish our practical explorations of how to encourage children to develop healthy emotions, and still have a nagging curiosity about the psychological theories of emotion that we have not reviewed here. For that curious reader part 2 of this book has been added.

Chapter 8 introduces a theoretical discussion. Because every book is built on assumptions and every author has basic commitments, chapter 9 scans the study of emotion in scientific psychology in terms of basic ideological underpinnings, and chapter 10 sketches the religious commitments that fund the views presented in this book.

The two sections of this book have been written so that they are independent of each other. A reader who is especially interested in theory might wish to begin with part 2 and read part 1 after it. That would pose no problem. The reader who is not interested in the more theoretical discussions of part 2 might elect to stop reading at the end of part 1. That would not mean that this reader would miss out on the conclusions to part 1.

Although the tone and focus of the two parts of this book are quite different, they have a common purpose. They are both written for parents, teachers, and other adults who, motivated by a spirit of Christian charity, wish to be constructive forces in the lives of children.

Living with Feelings

1

Familiar Features of Emotion

Nearly all adults, and most children as well, have some idea of what is meant by words like *anger, fear,* and *happiness.* Even children too young to recognize these words can distinguish an angry face from a sad one well enough to be wary of the one and friendly toward the other. Pull an ugly face at a five-month-old. In all likelihood you will get a very sober look in return. Who would deny that these words and these facial expressions have something to do with emotions or feelings—we will use these words interchangeably. Nevertheless, emotions or feelings are complex, mercurial, and evasive when we try to catch them with definitions.

Let's see if we can pin down our topic a bit with some simple questions. Have you ever had an emotion? Well, of course you have. You know what an emotion is. Try this question, then: What is an emotion? That's a different sort of question, isn't it? It is not as easy to answer. There are many things we know from experience, even though we cannot fully describe them.[1]

1. Children have minimal language skills until at least eighteen months of age. However, it would fly in the face of considerable evidence to say that they do not yet know anything from experience. For an overview of early intellectual development, see Jerome Kagan and Howard A. Moss, *Birth to Maturity* (New York: Wiley, 1962).

Let's start exploring emotion by recognizing and naming some commonplace characteristics of it.

Situation or Personality

Some emotions are very momentary, because they arise in a passing situation. For example, take John who is driving his car down a very steep hill only to discover halfway down that his brakes are not working. As John realizes his predicament, how does he feel? No doubt, he feels scared. It would be nothing short of amazing if under these conditions John felt amused or delighted.

Fear is the emotion that fits the situation, and thus we assume that John's being afraid is not a peculiarity of his own character. It is true that some persons may have no fear in finding themselves in John's predicament, but we would consider them exceptional. We might even question whether it is normal or healthy to feel no fear when there is an immediate threat to life and limb.

On the other hand, there are emotions that are marks of character. We speak of some people as being fearful and others as being fearless. It is one thing to say that John was afraid when his brakes failed; it is quite another thing to say that John is a fearful character. Implied in the latter remark is the assumption that persons have emotional constitutions that predispose them to some emotions and disincline them to others.

Identifying a person as being jolly, bad tempered, morbid, or patient refers to that person's temperament. Or, it may be that a person with a certain type of temperament tries to resist certain kinds of emotion. For example, a person who cannot tolerate anger may go to great lengths to avoid situations in which conflict could provoke anger. Therefore, the emotional predispositions that we identify with *temperament* we tend to see as being more durable than are emotional reactions that are tied to passing *situations*.

Situational emotions are not entirely separate from the character traits that predispose a person to certain kinds of emotion. Repeated experience of an emotional situation may form a habitual response. That's why it is easy to understand that a person whose life has been strewn with catastrophe is anxious. It is harder to understand why a person whose life has been easy would nevertheless have an anxious temperament.[2]

Both passing feelings and emotional habits are reflected in the body. Situational emotions occur along with noticeable changes in bodily states. When we are emotionally aroused, our bodies react in a pattern most often associated with stress. It is as though emotional excitement (whether that be anger, fear, or delight) prepares us to act.

The division of the human nervous system that regulates readiness for action is called the *sympathetic division of the autonomic nervous system.* When it is activated our hearts pound and blood is distributed rapidly throughout our bodies. Breathing increases, because we need plenty of oxygen if we are going to be active, and the pupils of our eyes grow larger to prepare us to be alert.

Functions of our bodies that are not needed during states of high emotion are slowed down by the sympathetic division of the nervous system. For example, digestion slows down or stops, because the energy that it takes to digest food may be needed for other activities when emotional reactions start to accelerate.

There is another system in the human body that is the partner of the sympathetic nervous system. This system, called the *parasympathetic nervous system,* returns the body to its normal state after emotions have passed. Were it not for this system, emotion would leave the body in a state of tension and high energy-consumption. The parasympathetic division of the nervous system regulates the relaxing of emotion.

Bodily manifestations of emotional stress are the basis for lie detectors. The assumption is that a person is under greater stress when telling a lie than when telling the truth. Thus, when an individual tells a lie and is emotionally stressed, the sympathetic nervous system is likely to be activated—increased heart rate, rapid breathing, and raised blood pressure, which the machine called a polygraph measures.

2. For a social psychological discussion of how impressions of persons are formed on the basis of actions and circumstances, see Edward Jones and K. Davis, "The Attribution Process in Person Perception," in *Advances in Experimental Social Psychology,* vol. 2 (New York: Academic, 1965) pp. 219–66.

Knowledge that emotional stress shows itself in bodily re-actions has been around for a long time. There is a story that many centuries ago in Britain, suspects being tried for crimes were made to eat dry bread and cheese. If they were stressed because of guilt, it was assumed they would have dry mouths and would not be able to chew and swallow the "truth sandwich."

There remains a great deal about the bodily effects of emo-tional reaction that has not been explained. Still less is known about the bodily effects of long-term emotional habits. But evidence is accumulating that stressful living habits can take their toll on the body in the form of stomach ulcers, headaches, skin irritations, muscular and postural problems, back pains, certain disturbances of heart patterns, and many other phys-ical complaints.[3]

Many common sayings suggest that temperament is mapped out in the body. We say of a depressed person, "He looks like he's carrying the world's woes on his shoulders," because the posture of persons who are unhappy does tend to make them look as if they are weighted down. Similarly, we may say of someone who is easily offended and prone to anger, "She has a chip on her shoulder." Raised shoulders are a feature of an aggressive or sparring stance.

Examples of the ways in which our bodies participate in emotion are too numerous to consider exhaustively here. How-ever, even the few examples we have considered remind us that emotions do not merely float around in our heads. Emo-tions are as much a part of us as our bodies are.

Owner or Observer

The ways we ordinarily refer to emotions reflect whether the emotions are our own or someone else's. Interview John about how he felt when the brakes of his car failed. He might tell you that he felt panicky, broke out in cold sweat, felt his heart pound, got a buzzing feeling in his head, and momen-tarily lost any sense of time so that what happened within a few seconds seemed to take several minutes with everything moving in slow motion.

3. For a review of research on stress, see Hans Selye, *The Stress of Life*, rev. ed. (New York: McGraw-Hill, 1976).

All of John's descriptions refer to inner, or subjective, experiences. We understand his subjective experiences by empathizing with them ourselves: We know how John feels because we can imagine feeling the same way, or can remember an occasion when we felt that way.

But when we are direct observers, we are less likely to describe emotions in terms of feelings and more likely to describe them in terms of how they seem to appear. So if we meet John getting out of his car just as he has managed to bring it to a stop by using the gears and the handbrake, we will see a pale, shaking person who has wide eyes and a trembling voice.

If, in response to our question about how he is, John tells us that he is fine, we might counter that he looks terrible and seems badly shaken. In other words, people's emotions display themselves through physical appearance, and we often assume that we know how those people feel based on how they look.[4]

Often the two sides of emotion—what we feel in ourselves and what we sense in others—seem to flow together so that they are barely distinguishable. When we see someone else's emotions, we may share in the emotion so that we not only see it but feel it.

We have all had the experience of sharing in someone's embarrassment. It can be amusing to watch an audience of parents at a musical recital in which their children perform. When an earnest young musician gets stuck in the middle of a piece, his stress and embarrassment are reflected on his parent's faces. They may blush with him and for him.

Emotion is social. We feel for, with, and in reaction to others. Doing this depends on emotional communication. Sometimes communication is deliberate, as it is, for example, when we tell someone about our emotions by describing them in words.

Here is an example of empathy. A few years ago I was sitting in the waiting area of a large international airport waiting for my flight. As I was paging through a magazine I noticed a large Italian family escorting a very elderly woman to the gate for a flight destined for Rome. Watching them I could not understand a word they said, but I could tell that it was a

---

4. The relationship between habitual emotional states and body posture is discussed in Alexander Lowen, *Bioenergetics* (New York: Penguin, 1975).

painful good-bye. My own throat felt tight while my attention was riveted on this very human scene.

Suddenly I noticed the woman sitting next to me take out a tissue to wipe her eyes and blow her nose. When she realized that I had noticed, she somewhat embarrassedly excused herself. "Isn't this silly? I don't even know them," she remarked. Well, if it was silly, then we were both being silly. But I suspect that what happened to us as spectators was quite natural. We didn't have to know the family or understand what they were saying in order to know what they were feeling. We knew the feelings they were having because we had had them, too. That's empathy.

Choice or Chance

Emotions may take hold of us without our choosing or anticipating them. If we return to the example of John, whose brakes failed when he was driving down a steep hill, it seems quite clear that his fear was not something he had anticipated. He would not choose it. The only control he could exercise in this chance situation was managing his fear once he already was gripped by it.

Quite in contrast to unexpected and unformed emotions, however, are other emotions that we are able to invite and cultivate. For example, I have a beautiful recording of a Mozart string quintet. I listen to it over and over again. As I listen to the harmony, rhythm, and movement of the violins, strong emotions are stirred within me. The more I have listened to that music the more familiar it has become, and the more nuanced my feelings are. Sometimes I select that piece of music from among the others to which I could listen because I want to use the music to call forth that set of feelings.

There are many ways we can choose emotions instead of leaving them to chance. One obvious way is to control the circumstances under which certain emotions are likely to be called forth. Consider this situation. When you try to do too many things in one short hour, you are likely to put yourself into a predicament in which you become impatient and angry with people.

Imagine that you are on your way to work trying to get

there on time, but you decide to stop off at the post office to mail a package. There you are in the post office, watching the large clock on the wall tick the precious minutes away, and you are at the end of a line that moves *very* slowly. Your irritation increases, because one person ahead of you has not bothered to look up a postal code in advance. The postal worker is not in a hurry. There is a parent with a restless youngster who will not behave, and this only adds tension to the situation.

Perhaps you are a person who can stand in the line at the post office and fume quietly without victimizing anyone else with your irritation. Perhaps you can walk out of the door and put the irritation away as though nothing has happened. But, what if you are a person who is not blessed with patience? Maybe you get hot under the collar, and once you get going in this emotional track, everything that follows adds to your irritability.

If you are a person who does not get over irritations quickly, the frustration may get pushed further along throughout your day. You are already irritated from the scene in the post office, and because now you are also late for work, your foul luck continues. You get stuck behind a slow driver. Your impatience mounts when you get to work and discover that you missed an important phone call because you were late.

The rest of the day follows suit, one irritation after the other. Finally, when the day is done, you go home, and the dog adds one last offense by tracking mud into the house. You lose your temper and kick the poor beast. It's embarrassing to admit where the buck stops.

What might we learn from this somewhat exaggerated example? A person who has difficulty handling irritations, and especially a person who tends to displace irritation by dumping it on someone else, would do well to avoid the circumstances that give rise to these ugly scenes. Exercising good judgment and not making the mistake of stopping off on the way to work again, especially when there are time pressures, would be one way of choosing emotions rather than leaving them to chance.

Another obvious way in which we can gain control of emotions is by reflecting on the situations in which they arise. Our understanding may not actually change events, but it may change our reactions to them. Imagine that you make an appointment to meet a friend at noontime. After you have spent an hour waiting, it becomes clear to you that your friend is not going to appear. You may feel hurt that your friend would think so little of your meeting. Or you may wonder if you have made an error of time, date, or place.

Suppose that the next day you call your friend to express your displeasure at being left waiting, and you learn that the reason your friend did not appear was that he was playing an arcade game and forgot your meeting. That's an insult. Your anger was justified, and finding out how flimsy your friend's excuse actually was, you may be even angrier than you were before.

But consider this alternative ending to the same story. Suppose that you call your friend and learn that just the hour before the time to meet, your friend got a call informing him that one of his children had been struck in the head by a baseball, and the injuries required that the child be placed in intensive care. In the distress of the situation your friend could think of nothing but the survival of his child, and could not bear to leave the child's side to make a phone call, even though he had not forgotten your meeting.

These two alternative ways of construing the reasons for your friend's absence do not change the original event: You were left waiting, your friend did not appear, and you felt uncomfortable at the time. But knowledge makes a difference. Finding out that your friend was playing in the arcades would make you feel angrier, but finding out about a family emergency would turn your anger to concern and sympathy. Therefore, what you know influences how you feel. Or, using more technical language, we say that there is a *cognitive* side to emotion. One major way of taking charge of emotions is to be sure that you have adequately filled in the cognitive side—an important step that follows your initial emotion.

Desirable or Undesirable

There are some emotions we work hard to have; there are other emotions we work hard to avoid. Most of us welcome delight. But to be only and always thoroughly delighted might lead to shallowness of personality. Nevertheless, to be delighted often is worth the risk. By contrast, revulsion is unpleasant. Things or events to which we respond with revulsion are noxious. We sense that we should not linger in their presence if we don't want to be corrupted or distressed by them. Revulsion is something we want to avoid.

What is it that makes an emotion desirable or undesirable? It cannot be the importance of the emotion, because even undesirable emotions, such as fear, are important. It would be dangerous to have no fear in the presence of a poisonous snake. Fear is a protection; it signals to us the need to proceed with caution. Unpleasant emotions are important and may serve us well under some circumstances.

Emotions signal something about the state of our well-being. Those which we experience as being desirable are those which signal that we are in a state that contributes to our good. Those which we experience as unpleasant are those which signal the need for a corrective. The signaling effect of emotion applies not only to our own well-being but also to the well-being of others. In fact, it reflects our relationship with them. We feel differently about the distress of our friends from that of our enemies.

The signaling function that emotions serve is tied in with actions. It is as though our emotions turn us toward certain actions and away from others. Those emotions that we experience as being undesirable tend to turn us away from their objects. For example, we try to move away from those things that we fear. In contrast, those emotions that we experience as being desirable tend to draw us toward their objects. For example, we try to be with persons whom we like.

In view of our first impulse to act hurtfully toward those who hate us, it strikes us as peculiar that Jesus would say we must love our enemies and do good to those who hate us (Luke 6:27). Our instincts are to barricade ourselves against our enemies or to destroy them, not to love them. But Jesus tells us to love our enemies by doing right by them even if we don't like them. Right action does not require that we deny our feelings. If we pause to reflect on the meaning of Jesus' advice, we begin to see that it is the way of wisdom, because he teaches that under the worst of circumstances we can be instruments for good.

Distressing emotions may signal trouble and may prompt us to act, but when we do act we need to consider more than the push of our emotions. We need to consider the results as well. For example, when we are angry our feelings signal to us that we are set in opposition to someone else. Something must be done. Our inclination to return insult for insult fans the flames of anger and creates a conflict in which the strong will win and the weak will lose. However, if either of us is weakened or crippled emotionally, we all lose, because the potential of someone God created for good purpose has been lost.

But when we express our anger in a way that moves toward resolution and peace, we do more than express our emotions. Genuine peacemaking (not just covering anger over) brings us back into a relationship with our neighbors that is more in line with what is wholesome for both of us. It is not in the spirit of Christ's teachings that the strong should win and the weak lose. It is the spirit of Christ's teachings that we should live together with peace and justice, each of us being able to do what is God's kind will for us. In this vision of the kingdom of righteousness there are no losers.

Although our emotions are woven in with our actions, they are counselors to our actions but not their dictators. Our emotions give us a strong sense of our condition; however, we must make insightful and responsible decisions when we act to alter our condition.

To act blindly according to the dictates of feelings is unwise. To ignore feelings as they point out to us the need to act is equally unwise. The way of wisdom is the way of integration. It is a return to harmony and balance that Christ's teachings hold up as an ideal. Both our feelings *and* actions need to be brought into balance with our intention to love our neighbors and be healthy, productive persons ourselves.

We began this chapter by reflecting on some common experiences with which we can easily associate the word *emotion*. From the many possible facets of emotion we observed these:

1. Our language about emotion refers both to predispositions of *character* and to qualities of specific *situations*
   that evoke emotional responses.
2. Our subjective experiences of emotions are on one side
   of a coin; on the other side are those signs of emotions
   that allow us to understand other persons.
3. Sometimes emotions occur apart from our choosing, but
   with understanding we can have more choice about the
   form our emotions take and the way we express them in
   action.
4. Both desirable and undesirable emotions are important
   signals. These signals counsel our actions, but they need
   not dictate our actions.

Once we take a look at some everyday emotional events, it
becomes clear that we already know a lot about emotion from
experience. In some sense each one of us is an expert because
we all have feelings. By taking time to look at emotions more
carefully we can have a deeper understanding of our feelings,
learn to talk about them more clearly, and take fuller responsibility for them. Furthermore, as we become more mature in
dealing with our own feelings we also will become better
emotional partners for children. That is a goal for this
discussion.

2

Goals for Emotional Growth

A young man in my neighborhood is training to compete in a triathalon. He doesn't take the day off if it rains. He figures it will help him emotionally to be familiar with competing under a variety of circumstances. That concern with adaptability is part of his conditioning. While he trains he sets goals for himself. He tells me that good athletic performance depends on being "up" for it. Being "up" clearly refers to his own state of mind and not to the rigors of the contest.

Emotional fitness also requires training. We can exercise our feelings and condition our reactions so that when it really counts we are ready to react in the most effective manner. But, can we actually set goals for emotional growth?

On the one hand we know that we cannot decide whether or not to have emotions. Some emotions we have whether we like them or not. For example, a speaker who has stage fright would rather not have that uncomfortable feeling, but not *wanting* to be frightened doesn't seem to make much difference.

On the other hand, just because some emotions seem to be spontaneous is not sufficient reason to conclude that they should be allowed to take whatever form they do apart from any attempt to control them. We probably cannot decide whether or not to have emotions, but we can shape the kinds of emotional habits we develop.

Like any sort of conditioning, emotional fitness takes some effort. By reflecting on our emotional habits we can begin to alter old patterns and develop new ones. Once we gain some insight into our emotional habits, we can actually seek out experiences that will help us retrain them. For example, we can work on expressing emotions accurately so that the ways we reveal our emotions synchronize well with our inner feelings. As our emotional expressions become clearer we are able to find allies who will understand our emotions with us and encourage us to handle our emotions in a healthy fashion.

As we learn to take responsibility for our own emotional habits, we can be a more positive force in helping our children live well with their emotions. When I hear the writer of Exodus predict that iniquity passes from those who hate the Lord to their generations after them, and that God shows steadfast love to generations of those who love him (Exod. 20:5, 6), I can't help but wonder if the effects of child rearing and the influence of parental example are not the means by which this prediction is made true.

No children deserve poor examples, but deserving or not, children whose parents display poor emotional patterns are in danger of repeating their parents' mistakes. Children whose parents provide them with good examples of healthy living are the recipients of a very special grace. Your children do not always do as you say, but it is very likely that they will do as you do. An example is a powerful motivator.

The influence of good models is exerted in many directions. Children learn emotional habits from parents and teachers, but sometimes parents and teachers also learn from children. Husbands and wives reciprocally influence each other. The model of wise and caring persons has tremendous influence in nurturing the emotional growth of persons who trust them to give counsel and leadership.

Some reflection on the meaning of experience may be helpful here. We often refer to persons as "having experience." For example, we speak of an experienced teacher, parent, politician, or leader. Referring to someone as experienced not only reflects what this person has done in the past, but also how

past events have built up and built out that person's awareness, sensitivity, and good judgment. We trust that people learn
from experience and that their experiences teach them how to
act effectively in the future.

We are shaped emotionally by the events we experience.
Through experience our emotions become more seasoned and
elaborate, and this may be for better or worse. We have some
choice of experiences as they occur; we can seek out some and
avoid others.

For persons whose attitudes are based on strong religious
traditions the question of the formation of others' emotional
habits and all its implications is especially important. For example, with the best of intentions many teachers and parents
believe that good children have "nice" emotions. Christian
parents may fortify their case by quoting this well-known
passage in Paul's writings about the fruits of the spirit:

> But the fruit of the Spirit is love, joy, peace, patience, kindness,
> goodness, faithfulness, gentleness, and self-control. Against such
> things there is no law (Gal. 5:22, 23).

Some time ago I was given a church-school tract that had
been prepared for children too young to read. It was designed
to help children reflect on Christian character. On one page
were several pictures of children: one was a child smiling and
holding a kitten very carefully, another was two happy children holding hands, a third was a child obviously having a
temper tantrum, and a fourth two children in a tug-of-war.
The church-school students were to circle the pictures of the
children who showed they love Jesus.

The message of this little set of pictures and the exercise is
a powerful, but in my opinion, unhealthy message. The impli-
cation is that children who love Jesus have "nice" feelings.
They laugh and smile, hold hands, feel generous, and are always sweet.

But do we really want every Christian child to be a Pol-
lyanna? When children get angry, feel jealous, get scared, frown,
or cry, is it a sign that they do not love Jesus? Isn't it really
the case that when children struggle with these difficult feelings, they especially need the assurance that Jesus loves them?
If we fall into the habit of thinking that pleasant emotions are

good and unpleasant emotions are bad, and if we consequently elect to cover up negative emotions rather than attend to them, learn from them, and grow from them, we lose integrity and become emotionally artificial.

Phony but nice emotions can hardly be the way of spiritual wisdom. When Donna's toddler swallowed drain cleaner, Donna was pale with fright. To be at ease in the face of threat is foolish. June and Ron went to visit their close friends whose six-year-old had died of leukemia. It was a very sad visit. Why shouldn't it have been? To minimize the situation would have been cruel. In the church-school class that David teaches, there is a child who had cigarette burns on his legs a few months ago. David reported it, but nothing happened. This week the same child has a bruised arm. David is enraged. He should be. At times it is quite fitting for devout Christians to be frightened, grief smitten, or enraged.

In reaction to an emphasis on saccharine goodness, some Christians have turned to another equally dangerous extreme. They conclude that emotions are what they are, and they make an idol of the freedom to express whatever they feel. There is, however, a vast difference between haphazardly expressing emotions and taking responsibility for emotions so that they can be healthy and whole. Let's take anger as our sample case.

Retaining anger and doing nothing about it almost never leads to a healthy conclusion. Unattended anger may turn into resentment or vengeance; denied anger that becomes disconnected from its original object may erupt against an innocent victim or be turned inward where it shows up as self-hatred, feelings of worthlessness, or depression.

When the Bible says, "Be angry but do not sin; do not let the sun go down on your wrath" (Eph. 4:26), it is pointing the way to health. The force of this scriptural advice is that we should see anger through to its conclusion. These wise words neither advise us to bury anger nor suggest that we spray it about at random and let it land where it may.

Buried anger chews at us from the inside. If we let it be, we harbor it like an untreated disease. But anger in the form of hit-and-run attacks, anger with no apparent explanation, outbursts from which no peacemaking follows, fiery displays that only serve to provoke greater and greater hurt in an uncontrolled volley of insults, all lead away from rather than toward re-establishing healthy feelings.

Healthy anger is anger that we accept as a signal of something gone wrong. It is anger we take seriously in terms of both cause and resolution. Healthy anger is not hidden but healed. Just as a pain denied cannot be treated, or a wound on which further blows are landed does not heal, so responsible anger is anger that we work on and with until it is no longer necessary, because that which provoked it is no longer a problem.

Admittedly, sometimes the solutions to anger are not so simple. They may take a long time, and sometimes complete resolution cannot be achieved. But even working toward, if not yet achieving, a resolution to anger helps to keep the emotion within a healthy range.

Therefore, if we are able to avoid both the extremes of artificial goodness and dangerous irresponsibility in expressing our emotions, we need to have goals for our own emotional growth. And once we have those goals in mind we have to keep working toward them if we want to stay emotionally healthy. Emotional fitness is like physical fitness. It takes maintenance. What then are those goals? We may begin by singling out three of them: richness, fit, and control.

Richness

Emotional health requires experiencing and expressing a wide variety or richness of feelings; but quantity of feeling by itself does not ensure richness. Some persons who appear to be extremely emotional are actually extremely impoverished, for they have only a limited range of emotional reactions to fit every type of occasion. These persons, while very emotional, are also immature. They are severely limited, because although they have emotions their emotions do not help them to deal with events in their lives effectively.

At one time I worked with a high school student, Philip, who had conflicts with his father. His father was a thoroughly angry person. Although Philip had problems of his own, they were compounded by the fact that in every one of their encounters his father had the same emotional response. It was brought home clearly when Philip had a motorcycle accident in which he received some minor injuries.

Any accident is upsetting, and it was to be expected that Philip's accident would set loose an array of feelings. Philip's injuries hurt, but he also felt foolish because the accident could have been prevented with some caution on his part. His mother felt worried about him. She cried because she was frightened by what could have happened, but she also was relieved that Philip's injuries had not been more severe than they were. But Philip's father was angry, just plain angry about everything.

Dad felt angry because Philip had not been careful, because he had not been wearing his helmet when the accident occurred, because the motorcycle had been costly and now was damaged. He was angry with the road commission for not banking the curve better and for not providing better lighting. The hospital staff got their turn at being the object of this man's anger because he thought they were not attending to his son's injuries quickly enough in the emergency unit. Philip's mother was ridiculed for being so silly as to cry.

Philip's angry father, it seemed, could respond to every aspect of his son's accident with only one emotion, because it was the only way he knew of reacting to any emotional situation. He was an emotional monotone. *Anger* was the only vocabulary of feeling he had.

Unfortunately, the emotional poverty of Philip's father set loose a scramble of confused emotions in his wife and son. His wife's fears took on an echo of embarrassment because she felt foolish as well as misunderstood. Philip felt hurt because his father apparently cared more about the motorcycle than about him.

Tangled emotion was typical of Philip's family. What happened so obviously in this one instance had often happened before. They all ended up feeling edgy and alienated, each one alone with a mass of confusing feelings and having no sense of how to resolve them and get back onto solid footing with each other.

Philip's father, while an obvious case of emotional poverty, is not so different from the rest of us. We all have certain areas of emotional response that are closed off and for which we substitute other habitual emotions that are less honest and less healthy. Each of us, if we reflect on our emotional habits, can probably identify certain emotions that we do not allow ourselves to have and others that we use more often than is appropriate.

There are a lot of reasons why people become emotionally narrow. Sometimes gaps in emotion are products of long-standing family patterns. For example, some families do not allow open expression of appreciation and affection, because they have unspoken rules about sentimentality. Other families do not allow the expression of anger, because it does not look nice. Still other families maintain pretentions of courage, because they place a high priority on always being strong and in control.

While there may be no intentional ill will on the part of families who discount one or another kind of emotion, family habits of denying certain emotions have unfortunate consequences. Family members learn to substitute allowable emotions for those which they do not allow themselves to express.

We all know parents who obliquely express devotion to their children by grousing about how much they do for their children. They compliment their children by calling them rascals. It may be entertaining when Erma Bombeck does this, but this habit does not wear well in families.

One can only guess what is really behind admiring complaints. It could be embarrassed affection, but it could also be rejection. It is not surprising that children in such families learn to return admiration by returning complaints. It's safer that way, but it gets awfully complicated and isn't very satisfying.

Society, too, encourages gaps in the range of permissible emotions. Many men do not think they have permission to be sad or afraid. Those men who give in to such pressures may even succeed in deleting these feelings from their emotional range. Nevertheless, sooner or later they have to deal with sad or frightening events, or at least with sad and frightened persons.

To cover the gap in their own range of emotions, what can these men do but fill in with the emotions they are allowed to have? As a result, men who do this will be awkward in sad and frightening situations. They will not be able to show empathy, and in all likelihood will add insult to injury by failing to understand.

Inasmuch as we go along with the unhealthy patterns society imposes on men we force them to be heroes, but they become our emotional victims. We keep them emotionally limited. Little do they realize that their efforts to appear strong weaken their effectiveness with persons closest to them.

Women, too, can be victimized by social expectations.[1] Anger is the emotion that many women consider is not allowed to them. They think that anger makes them ugly, silly, or unladylike. While it is probably true that anger does not make a person attractive, neither do weak substitutes for anger such as self-pity or depression. And certainly the confusion created by emotional crisscrossing does not lead to clear and healthy relationships.

Pointing out patterns of emotional poverty is only a first step. If we truly wish to be good guardians of emotional health we must take seriously the possibility of turning around habits of emotional poverty and moving in the direction of emotional richness. It will take time and awareness to change societal patterns. The place to begin is in those domains where we have personal contacts: the family, the workplace, the classroom, and with friends.

It is especially with children that the most promising possibilities for emotional enrichment present themselves. Emotionally rich adults also enrich children's feelings, because at least to some extent children learn the range of their emotions by sharing in the experiences of adults. We will explore these possibilities in the following chapters.

Once we take seriously the potential for helping children develop emotional richness, we also discover that children can become our teachers. Children can express in a simple way those emotions that adults, because they are more complex, are less skilled in handling. Children, because of their lack of experience, are not as fixed in unhealthy habits as many adults are, nor are children as crafty as adults in hiding their true feelings and substituting others.

1. For a helpful discussion of anger, see Carol Tavris, *Anger: The Misunderstood Emotion* (New York: Simon and Schuster, 1983).

Some adults may find the suggestion that children become our emotional teachers a threatening proposal. These adults may fear that the goal of emotional richness will become an excuse for an emotional free-for-all and that adults will become victims of an emotional tyranny exercised by children. What these wary adults fail to recognize is that it is possible to appreciate emotion without becoming slavish to it.

By recognizing the emotional vitality of children we become positive in our guardianship of them and more effective participants in their feelings; however, we need not get caught up in emotionally romanticizing children or assuming that their emotions are fresh and good while those of adults are twisted and bad. Concluding such would only replace an old and undesirable notion of emotion with a new one that is equally undesirable.

Thus far we have discussed the implications of emotional poverty versus emotional richness for the individual, but emotional richness also has important implications for relationships. Persons who themselves lack emotional range are not able to understand the emotions of others. Understanding depends on empathy, which is the ability to imagine what it is like to stand in another's place.

Empathy involves understanding someone else's feelings by remembering or imagining how it feels to be in the same circumstance. If we are able to empathize with someone else's feelings we more than likely are also able to understand their actions.

When we refuse to have certain emotions for ourselves, we are unable to understand and deal wisely with those same emotions in others. Once again, an example can help us explore what this means. Many children go through stages of being timid or shy. Sometimes they are so overwhelmed by their feelings of uncertainty and fear that they freeze in social situations.[2] Adults who have learned to deny their own feelings of timidity in order to be able to function well socially have difficulty understanding children's shy feelings.

Empathizing with shy children requires calling forth in our-

2. For a careful discussion of stranger anxiety, see J. Kagan, "Emergent Themes in Human Development," *American Scientist* 64 (1976): 186–96.

selves those same feelings of fear and uncertainty that the children have. But if fear and uncertainty are among those emotions that we will not allow ourselves to feel, it is unlikely that we can understand shy children. We may mistake a shy child's terror as a sign that the child is stubborn, or mistake awkward behavior as the child's gesture of defying us personally.

If an adult interprets a child's social fear as an act of defiance, the adult's attempts to deal with the child's difficulty will be off the mark. Confronting defiance only further intimidates the frightened child.

What the frightened child needs is some reassurance that an adult will be ready to offer support, that the child will not be left alone or deserted without any familiar persons to rely on, and that someone else can understand that it is uncomfortable but not bad to be shy. In other words, the *shy* child needs help to build feelings of strength; this is exactly what the *defiant* child does not need.

Examples such as the one just given could be multiplied *ad infinitum*. The point here, though, is a simple one. It takes emotional richness—a wide range of emotional experience—to understand the emotions of others and to help others deal constructively with their emotions. It takes a developed vocabulary and practice in expressing feelings to communicate well on an emotional level.

It is important at this point to remind ourselves that emotional richness is not our only goal. We began by setting three goals for emotional growth: richness, fit, and control. By taking all three of these goals seriously we can begin to discover what it might mean that in addition to setting our emotions free we want to cultivate and form them constructively. And so we must move on to consider how we may judge whether our emotions are fitting.

Fit

Healthy emotions are solidly connected to and synchronized with events; they are fitting. There is a sense in which emotions may be true or false. Just as the truth of a statement depends, in part, on how well it corresponds to an event, so the truth of an emotion depends on how appropriate it is to an event.

A pleasant feeling in the face of a horrid event is false, and despair in the presence of great possibilities is equally false.

Emotion may be spoken of as true or false because emotions are a form of knowledge. We often speak of them as if they are a private fiction or a swirl of confused feelings contained within us. But emotions are a response to *real* events. They are triggered by the way we have perceived or know past events in our lives, and then they become part of our store of feelings that signal to us what needs to be done.

Let us take here as our example the reaction of fear. When we respond to an event with fear, not only do we have a prior subjective experience to which we may refer with the expression "I feel afraid," but our bodies also prepare for escape. In chapter 1 we noted that certain changes take place in our sympathetic nervous systems when we become afraid. Our hearts beat faster, our rate of breathing increases, and the energy sources of our bodies prepare to be set loose if we need to expend them to defend ourselves.

The evidence of bodily changes involved in emotion shows that emotions are not just ideas. Emotions involve not only how we think and how we feel, but also how we act. All of these in turn reflect how we understand events around us, and how we are involved in those events. Furthermore, past experiences of emotion also shape how we react to present events. Thus our emotional experiences have long-term consequences for our relationships with the world and other persons.

Emotions mediate the continuous series of exchanges that we carry on with the world, but while mediating these exchanges our emotions do not control them. An element of decision is involved in how we emotionally react to events. Sometimes the decision is a conscious one.

For example, after telling the newspaper carrier at least six times to throw the newspaper on the porch where it will stay dry and not on the steps where it will get wet in rain and snow, Louise feels very irate when she once again picks up a sodden newspaper. Probably she has little choice about whether or not to *feel* irritated; she does feel irritated, and that is all there is to it. But is that really all there is to it?

Even in situations in which Louise cannot help but feel angry, does she not have some choice about how to *express* that anger? Furthermore, can she not choose how to act so that she will not have to deal with anger over and over again about the same thing?

Perhaps Louise will choose to wait until she sees the newspaper carrier throwing a newspaper at her steps on the next day, and then she will loose her anger by dashing out of the front door with a shrieking sermon. Or she may calmly devise a way to make sure that the incident will not be repeated. She will tell the carrier that she does not want any more newspapers delivered. Or, she might alternatively decide that she does not want to be without a newspaper, and she may tell the carrier that if she gets another spoiled paper she will not pay what she owes when it is time to collect. She may even decide to temper her irritation once more with patience and try to find out why the carrier cannot remember what to Louise seems like such a simple request. Now, that's quite a range of possibilities.

One of the most difficult things for us to remember when we are suddenly overwhelmed by a powerful surge of emotion is that there are other possible ways to deal with any situation than our initial emotions suggest. Take the example of Louise's newspaper carrier once again and imagine that she decides to talk with this seemingly forgetful kid.

Louise wants to find out why her newspaper carrier is careless, but in the course of the conversation she finds out that the youngster has more problems than just getting a dry paper to her house. Louise finds out that if a disgruntled patron calls to complain that a newspaper was not delivered, the child's parents react with a harsh punishment.

The carrier, with a glimmer of pride, tells Louise that every paper has been delivered to the right house every day for six weeks and that there have been no punishments during that whole time. This seems like progress grown from admirable effort.

Finding herself sympathetic with the child who earlier had irritated her, Louise decides to try teamwork. She suggests that she put a little yellow ribbon around the post of her porch to remind the carrier to aim for the porch. Much to her delight, the scheme works. Now at the end of this long process we can quite legitimately say that, in addition to having a dry newspaper and a new friend, Louise has expressed her original anger and brought it to a good end.

Solving a problem that provokes anger is also a fitting expression of anger. It is an example of how the fitting expression of an emotion serves as a desired corrective. Fitting expression *intensifies* those emotions which make our lives and relationships full, and fitting expression *reduces* those emotions which signal that our lives and relationships are not satisfactory.

For us to have fitting emotions and fitting expression of them requires that we have knowledge. It requires that we learn to understand our own emotions and the emotions of others in the contexts of their occurence. Fitting emotions are those which accurately (in this sense, truly) reflect events, and they are emotions which point us toward actions that will allow us to live most constructively with others.

Lest we think the example of Louise's newscarrier is too idealistic, let us consider one other possible outcome of the anger Louise felt at once again finding a wet newspaper. Suppose the next time she sees the newspaper carrier she goes out the front door of her house and says she would like to talk about getting her paper delivered in readable condition.

It turns out that the carrier is a cocky and contrary character who tells Louise to get lost and writes her off with a vulgar gesture. Suppose Louise then responds by saying that she does not wish to have the newspaper delivered under such circumstances, and that she also intends to report this behavior by calling the carrier's supervisor. Having stated her anger and her intentions, Louise turns around and sternly walks back into her house. This reaction would seem to be an appropriate response to an intentional insult.

What would be fitting behavior in the case of the first example would not be fitting in the second. It would not be wise to respond to an affront with kindness any more than it would be wise to respond to an honest mistake by being unnecessarily stern. Fitting emotions are synchronized in an appropriate and responsive fashion with the emotions and intentions of others and with the best possible outcomes of the situation.

In discussing appropriate emotion it is important to recognize that many of our emotional reactions occur in the context of social relations. Just as we need to know what our own feelings are, and just as we need to be able to read the feelings of others in order to act appropriately toward them, so it is important that we learn to accurately communicate our emotions to others. Our emotional expressions are cues to others about how they may most fittingly deal with us.

Earlier we discussed how our subjective experiences of emotion and the bodily states that accompany them may prompt us to act in certain ways. In a somewhat parallel fashion, our expressions of emotion serve others as cues that point to how they may act toward us. Let us take here as our example the expression of grief or sadness.

We sometimes make the mistaken assumption that persons who do not express their grief are especially heroic. But there is another side to this heroism. The person who will not express grief is also refusing to be comforted. It is the *expression* of grief that invites comfort. When the exchange of grief and comfort is stifled, the grieved one may feel desperately lonely and the potential comforter terribly helpless.

The sad consequences of unexpressed and unfit emotion often have an ongoing effect. When emotion is not given fitting expression it often runs stuck. Because the emotion is not moved toward resolution it lingers on.

In families, the damaging effects of heroic silence often become apparent when it is too late. For example, it is one thing for a wife to be told by her husband that he feels personally insulted because she was late today and he had to wait for her, even though he also was very busy and his time was as valuable as hers. If the grievance is today's grievance, then the regret can also be today's regret, and resolutions can be made to not repeat the insult.

But sometimes, for the sake of false heroism, a spouse may decide to say nothing about an aggravation and instead just steam about it inwardly for a while. Imagine the distress when after twenty years a husband says to his wife, "For twenty years I've been standing around waiting for you, and you've never been on time. I know exactly what you've thought of me. It all adds up to nothing."

Each time his wife is late, this husband feels the intensity of twenty years of anger, and once it bursts forth she cannot acknowledge guilt in proportion to his accusation, because she feels deceived by his silence. She can only reply by saying, "Why didn't you ever say anything? Why did you just let me go on doing something that bothered you so much? Now after all these years how can I ever undo all of that insult?"

What our example illustrates is that silence may be unfitting because it is misleading. If we are concerned about moving forward in the course of our own emotional health and in the growth of emotionally healthy relationships, then we need to develop a sense of what constitutes fitting emotion and appropriate expression.

Fitting emotion can best be learned by experience; we can learn by observing those patterns of expression in ourselves that help to move our relationships in the direction of harmony and respect, of cooperation and concern. As our emotions become increasingly honest and fitting, we move closer to the real meaning of what it is for us to love our neighbors emotionally.

By learning how woven through with emotion our experiences and relationships are, we are naturally brought to a third goal for emotional growth. It is emotional control.

Control

Over the last several decades, self-help psychology has gone through an antitraditional and antiauthoritarian phase. One of the tenets of this approach to emotional health has been an emphasis on self-expression that has discredited any form of holding back emotion for the sake of conforming to the will or wishes of others.

This message concerning emotional health has fit in well with the more general ethos of a society in which each person is supposed to be free to pursue his or her own life, liberty, and happiness. While the protection of basic freedoms need not and ought not be questioned, the exercise of these freedoms in our society deserves our consideration as a preface to our discussion of what healthy emotional control means.

The highest ideals of freedom are grounded in the belief that persons of various kinds have their own visions of what life, lived at its best, ought to be like; that a life lived in conformity with one's noblest visions leads to happiness; and that everyone should have the liberty to pursue such happiness. Furthermore, because it cannot be assumed that everyone else's vision of life conforms to yours or mine, and because you and I cannot assume that everyone else can appreciate our vision, we all live under similar restraints not to impose our ways on others. Abiding by these restraints, we all in turn derive the freedom to live as we wish or believe that we must.

Somewhere along the way, unfortunately, we have lost a sense of the significance of enduring visions—living by principles that guide us in many situations—and in the place of this ideal has come a more infantile notion quite similar to "having your own way." Thus, we have come to think of freedom as getting what we want, acting as we wish, and saying what we feel, even if all of these are spawned only by momentary impulses. In addition, we have come to think of freedom as being sure that we will have minimum consequences for acting on our own impulses—at least minimum negative consequences.

It is not surprising that in the context of such a mentality the notion of emotional self-control is not a favored one. Given these assumptions about freedom, emotional control could only mean that one person's impulses are dominated by the impulses of another. If that were the case, then every one of us could quite understandably argue, "Why is what anyone else wants any better than what I want?"

Faced with the dilemma of either being arbitrarily controlled by others or of being left to their own impulses, many people have concluded they would prefer their own way. Thus, we have become a society of people "busy doing their own thing," "getting what they want," and assuming that this is the best life can be.

Judging by the emotional health of the general population, the experiment has not worked. Our society has produced many impulsive and visionless persons who assume that they are free, but who really feel that they are empty. They cannot understand why, when they can do pretty much as they want, they still are not happy. The myth of freedom has convinced them that there should be something inside of them that will be satisfying and satisfied if it can just be expressed, but when they search inside themselves they find there is nothing more than whimsy.

Today many people are longing for what now seems like an old-fashioned value, a cause, a goal, or an ideal that could be the lodestar of their lives. The emotional evidence of their predicament is their feeling of fragmentation. Their emotions seem to be like echoes without original sounds. They lack a center; they have no direction.

But to have emotional control we must have direction, a deep purpose in life that gives it continuity, something on which to center ourselves. Then and only then is it possible to judge the quality of our emotions. If our lives have a purpose and a direction, we are able also to look at the ongoing patterns of our lives and honestly assess whether who we are and how we are is what we ought to be.

In order to be healthy persons, our deepest sense of direction must be reflected in our emotions. If it is, our emotions will also serve to show us when we are moving in a fitting direction and when we are being diverted from it.

Our emotions express what is most important to us. For example, if ambition dominates a person's life, that person's emotions will also come to be dominated by and will serve that ambition. Or similarly, in the case of persons for whom being liked is most important, this motive bends and shapes their emotions. On an emotional level this is what is meant by the statement that from the heart come the issues of life (Prov. 4:23).

There is a still more profound level at which we may be aware of the relation of emotions to our deepest commitments. These commitments cannot be purely arbitrary, for our deepest commitments do not remain locked away within us. They are part and parcel of our motives and actions, and these in turn have consequences.

Although all of us have some freedom to shape and influence our own lives and the lives of others around us, it is nevertheless also the case that all of us live subject to what is divinely intended for us. If our lives express a self-transcending will—

God's will, with his grace added—we are able to enjoy the gifts of peace and joy and love.

When we violate the divine will for us, this, too, has real consequences for us and for others. Thus, for example, we may be dominated by ambition, but if this is contrary to our spiritual well-being, the acting out of our ambitions will cause damage in our lives and in the lives of others. And this will be reflected in our emotions.

It should be clear, then, that what is meant here by emotional control has very little to do with containing, stifling, or denying emotion. Controlling emotions is not a matter of *locking* them up, it is a matter of *following* them up wisely so that our feelings, our relationships, our actions, and our perceptions move toward greater and greater integrity. Emotional wholeness is part of a bigger picture. It is a gift given to persons who have the courage to live a life bound together by grace.

The goals for emotional growth that we have been reflecting on here are not three entirely separate goals. They are each firmly tied in with the others. As our emotional lives gain in richness, we are enabled to be more emotionally fitting, and this in turn is part of what it means to exercise emotional control. At the same time, the effort to be emotionally fitting and to extend our emotional lives as they become enriched is directed by our deepest commitments, which shape our lives in their entirety. What we seek in all of this is emotional wisdom.

The exercise of emotional wisdom requires that each of us continually reflects on a number of crucial questions. What is the purpose of my life? How can this be reflected in the way I act upon my emotions? What do my emotions and the emotions of others tell me about my motives, actions, and relationships? Are they in keeping with what I believe is the divine will for me? Emotional wisdom is, finally, spiritual wisdom.

3

Living with Children's Emotions

When we reflect on the emotional growth of children we must assume for ourselves the point of view of guardians who wish to be as wholesome and effective as possible in forming the emotional lives of children. The goals we envision for our own emotional development are also goals we may have for children, but we must remember that children are at a different stage of growth than we are. Consequently, there are some additional considerations in dealing with children and in trying to nurture their emotions.

Helpful adults can contribute much to children's emotional richness, emotional fit, and emotional control. We are certainly conscious of how children need our help when their situations are most extreme. How does an adult help a child frightened by illness, griefstricken by a grandparent's death, jealous of a sibling, or timid and insecure at school?

Faced with emotionally charged situations we sometimes wish we could simply take control of children's feelings. But in reality, the best we can do is join children in their feelings and help them along as partners working on the same problems. In fact, if we could save our children from all intense emotion, we would be depriving them.

It is easy to make the mistake of thinking that emotions mark only extraordinary events, because when emotions are most unusual, extreme, or troublesome we are most aware of them. However, in many small and unnoticed ways we are living with and expressing emotions all the time.

There is an interesting connection between conversation and emotion. Adults and children speak with each other many times each day, but when this communication becomes especially important, we refer to it as "talking something over."

However, it is the children and adults who talk with each other about ordinary events who are best prepared to talk about extraordinary or significant events. But when the skills of communication have not been exercised in simple ways, they are often not well enough developed to bear the strain of a situation that is complicated and stressful.

On many occasions I have worked with parents who were bewildered by the fact that their child went to a teacher, a neighbor, or an older sibling for help in dealing with a crisis. These parents were upset because their child did not come to them. What they did not understand is that children go for emotional help to persons with whom satisfying contact has already been established. They will not believe a parent who says, "I'm always here if you need me," but who by actions says, "Don't bother me with little stuff."

Adults then, parents and others, become children's emotional partners and play changing roles in the children's emotional development. Furthermore, as emotional contacts between children and adults accumulate over time, both partners develop versatility in the avenues through which they communicate emotionally with each other. We will explore four of these avenues through which adults make emotional contact with children: messages beyond words, the power of example, emotional partnerships, and the gift of guidance.

Messages Beyond Words

Emotional communication with children begins long before they understand language or speak their first words. An infant's response to emotion is evident during the first months of its life. According to some observers the basics of emotional communication are apparent within minutes of birth, at least in those cases where the shock and trauma of birth can be kept to a minimum.

Because of the sensitivity and alertness of newborns, birthing rooms are now designed with low lights and sound-absorbing materials, so that the infants are not bombarded by glare and noise in the first few minutes after birth. It is also, in part, for this reason that medications that dull infant alertness are avoided.[1]

Babies' pre-language displays of emotion and adults' unspoken displays of emotion come in many forms. They may be exhibited in facial expression, posture and gesture, and tone of voice. Just to refresh our memories about something we all know, let's consider each of these.

Facial expression. Babies are born with a remarkable ability that directs their attention to faces. At one time it was thought that infants can only see a blur of lights and colors for the first weeks after birth. More recently, researchers exploring infant vision have concluded that, within a very narrow range, newborns can see very clearly.

The portion of clear vision in the infant's visual field is that area about nine to eleven inches from the tip of the baby's own nose. When a newborn is nursing, its mother's face is approximately nine to eleven inches away from the tip of the baby's nose.[2] Although we can only speculate about why a baby's sight is designed as it is, the limits of newborn vision do have some remarkable consequences.

Because babies tend to look most attentively at objects within a close and clear range, their attention seems to be especially directed at human faces. Objects closer than nine to eleven inches and objects farther away than this—for example, objects across the room—are not as distracting as they might be if they were clearly in focus. By the way its vision is designed, a baby's attention is drawn to that human being to whom the little one needs to become attached. This attach-

1. Prominent among physicians advocating change in birthing procedures was M. H. Klaus. See M. H. Klaus and J. H. Kennell, *Maternal-Infant Bonding: The Impact of Early Separation or Loss on Family Development* (St. Louis: C. V. Mosby, 1976). Best known advocate of "gentle birth" is the French obstetrician Frederick Leboyer.

2. For a detailed presentation of infant visual abilities, see T. G. R. Bower, *Development in Infancy* 2d ed. (San Francisco: W. H. Freeman, 1981).

ment is essential if the baby is to develop normal behavior socially and emotionally.

But babies do much more than merely observe human faces; they reflect emotions themselves. Emotions are mapped out on babies' faces from birth, facial expressions adults identify as contentment, distress, and even disgust. By four to six weeks of age babies respond to a smile with a smile. And between three and six months of age many babies engage in exchanges of facial expressions with adults during which the infant imitates the adult and the adult imitates the infant almost as though they are carrying on a conversation without words.[3]

Most of the research that explores the signaling of emotion between children and adults has focussed on the interactions between children and their mothers. It seems that many mothers are very keen in understanding the unspoken language of emotion, and intuitively steer their children toward certain emotional expressions and away from others.

Some research suggests that mothers use a narrower range of emotions with boys than with girls. This may contribute to the greater skill at understanding emotion that females at every age level demonstrate compared with their male age mates.[4]

For the sake of our discussion it is significant to note that research on early facial expression indicates that emotional expression in infants is spontaneous, but also that it can be formed. Children are born with emotions, as far as we can tell, and they express them in response to important persons with whom they interact.

While it seems to be the case that infants have emotions independent of the ability of adults to elicit them, it also seems to be the case that as time goes on, the emotional exchanges between infant and adult encourage certain kinds of emotional expression and discourage others.

Posture and gesture. As children develop they gain increasing mastery of their bodies. Some of the major milestones are

3. See T. G. R. Bower, "Social Development" in *Development in Infancy*.

4. In the literature on emotion and non-verbal communication, females at every age level (as a group) seem to show greater skill and accuracy in interpreting unspoken cues. Whether this is a culturally formed skill, has something to do with brain organization, or is in any way innate is widely debated.

rolling over, sitting up, crawling, standing, walking, and running. There is, however, another line of development that is equally important, and that is the development of expressive skills. The emotional messages displayed by facial expression are also displayed by children's gestures and bodily posture. These expressions are called body language.

Let's consider some examples of the way children, and also adults, express emotion without words. Consider the child who draws his head down to his shoulders, looks down or to the side in a way that makes his face less visible, draws his hands and arms across his body, or covers his face with his hands.

What is such a child saying by these gestures? This is a child who is cowering because of fear, whose whole body is engaged in self-protection and withdrawal. It would be surprising, indeed, to find a smile on this child's face. The same emotional expression of fear that is displayed in this child's body would most likely also be mapped on his face.

Consider by comparison a child whose shoulders are drawn back, whose chest is thrust forward, whose hands are thrust out ahead of her body or to the side, whose face is clearly visible, and whose gaze is deliberately directed at you. This child's posture makes an aggressive statement, and on her face you would expect to see an expression of anger or of determination. Emotionally speaking, we do not just *have* bodies, we *are* our bodies. Our emotions take hold of us bodily.

Most of us read cues of gesture and posture in others better than we realize, and most of us also give signals more obviously and with greater accuracy than we realize. Children are less skilled than adults at putting words to things, but on the other hand, many of them are less inhibited than adults in showing their feelings through facial expression, gesture, and posture.

Tone of voice. Psycholinguists—persons who scientifically study language—have teased apart the ingredients of speech and in so doing have discovered that our voices do much more than produce words. We often think of speech as word production—something on the order of an audible typewriter. But to gain a sense of how much our tones of voice alone tell, we need only try to imitate robot or machine language. Then we see that it is nearly impossible for us to speak meaningful sentences without having our voices rise and fall, without having the texture and tempo of our speech sing along with our words.

The melody of our voices conveys much of the force of what we say. Children learn to play with the melodies of speech before they speak their first words. In the last half of their first year, for example, babies babble in patterns that can be distinguished as questions, commands, or straight-out declarations.

This same melodic quality of the human voice is a critical ingredient in communicating emotion. Consider for a moment how our voices rise and fall when we say, "This is disgusting." Compare this melody of voice to the contrasting melody that accompanies the statement, "Oh, what a wonderful surprise!" A statement about disgust is made with a closed throat and in a low tone; a statement of delight is made with an open throat and a light tone.

Voices communicate ease or tension, openness or rejection, affirmation or disapproval, warmth or chilliness, contact or disconnection, and many other subtle messages that reveal our emotions. The muscular and postural shifts that are required of the voice mechanism to produce the melody of speech are similar to the muscular and postural patterns that shape our facial expressions and body postures.

Children are remarkably sensitive to the expressions of the human voice. By the time they reach school age, most children can imitate the melody of anger, of fear, of delight, and of many other emotions. It is quite fascinating to ask a child to speak an emotional message with teeth together and mouth closed in a humming speech. For example, try to imitate the following dialogue using a humming speech:

Child: May I have a piece of candy?

Adult: No, it's almost time for lunch.

Child: But, I want a piece of candy.

Adult: No, you may not have one.

Child: Please?

Adult: No, absolutely not, and that's that. Don't ask again. I'm getting impatient.

Most school children can do humming speech as well as you can. It is nothing short of amazing how very accurately and at what a young age most children can sound out such a dialogue. They know the tones of voice that accompany the emotional quality of such utterances. They understand these messages because they send and receive them continually when they engage in speech.

I am struck sometimes by how adults frame communications with children in such a way as to break down the communication. A schoolteacher whose voice has a patronizing tone and a parent whose voice has a perennial tone of distrust are sending strong messages to children. They are surprised when children's responses are not positive and cooperative, but they are surprised only because they do not realize the way in which tone of voice may invite resistance.

If we are to carry on quality contact with children in the domain of emotional communication, we need to become alert to the subtleties of communication. We need to be well-tuned to their unspoken messages, and we need to be alert to our own as well.

Following are three exercises to help you to become sensitive to unspoken messages. The first exercise helps you become alert to children's messages. Think of a child whose behavior you do not understand and then try to imitate that child. Imitate the child's facial expression; imitate the child's posture; walk across the room the way this child would walk. Say something in the tone of voice with which the child often speaks. Finally, ask yourself what state of mind you would be in if you yourself were really looking, speaking, and acting that way. Sometimes mimicking provides clues to the mistakes we make in identifying a child's feelings. It is easiest to overlook in the child's behavior the emotions we ourselves are least likely to admit to or to express publicly.

Again, think about the various facets of that child's behavior one at a time: voice, posture, facial expression. Do they fit together, or are they contradictory? Is it possible that the child covers up one emotion with another that is more acceptable? For example, do some of the child's messages display anger, but others fear? Does the child cover up insecurity by acting tough, or cover anger with indifference?

This second exercise helps you become aware of the unspoken messages that you send. Act out the way in which you typically behave in dealing with children. Notice the tone of your voice. What does it convey? Look in a mirror and try to see your facial expression. What do you do with your eyes? Do you look at or away from children? Do you allow your eyes to meet theirs? What is your posture, your gestures, your gait?

Now ask yourself how you would react to a person presenting this same image to you, to see if your behavior toward children will invite the response that you wish. In other words, if you were the child, what would be the demeanor of a person to whom you would most likely respond in the way you actually wish children would act toward you? Can you imitate the demeanor that would get your desired response? How does this compare with your present actions?

The third exercise suggests ways to break through barriers to emotional contacts. Sometimes we cannot make contact with a child because the child's demeanor and our own demeanor clash. If the disparity is great enough, the child may close us off and refuse to give us enough attention to even begin communicating. Sometimes it helps to bend to the child's feelings by mirroring them back with voice, gesture, or posture. For example, it is very hard for a sad child to respond to an adult who approaches him with a broad smile, a bouncy voice, and the energy of a cheerleader. It is much easier to admit sadness to an adult whose voice, face, or posture says that this is someone who also knows what sadness is.

There are, of course, many other ways in which we can sharpen our awareness of children's emotions. But, in the final analysis, nothing teaches us as well how to communicate with children as the experience of doing so. Children sense very quickly if adults are genuinely interested in them, and most children respond quickly to adults who take them seriously.

The Power of Example

When children learn a language they depend on the example of others who already speak that language. This is not to suggest that language learning is nothing more than imitation, but there is no doubt about the fact that imitation is one among other important factors.

Learning how to express emotion appropriately is also learned, at least in part, through example. Thus, it is not surprising that we often observe similiar emotional habits among members of the same family. Some families express affection in a teasing and humorous way; other families express it more seriously. Some families tolerate noisy expressions of anger; others only allow anger to be expressed in silent disapproval.

A very fine portrayal of the power of example appears in a children's story by Dorothy Canfield Fisher. It is the story of a fragile and finicky little orphan girl, Betsy, who is adopted by her warmhearted country cousins, the Putneys. Betsy finds that her cousins do not fuss about the things she had learned to fuss about. They are quiet and undemonstrative people, but they are also solid and loving.

Through the course of Betsy's stay with the Putneys, another needy child is taken in by the family. This child, little Molly, becomes Betsy's protégé. In celebration of Betsy's birthday the family goes to the fair. Little Molly is so impressed that she insists they are celebrating her birthday, too, although it is still six weeks away.

> This made Betsy feel like laughing, but observing that the Putneys only looked at each other with the faintest possible quirk in the corners of their serious mouths, she understood that they were afraid that Molly's feelings might be hurt if they laughed out loud. So Betsy tried to curve her young lips to the same kind and secret mirth.[5]

What the simple little story of Betsy portrays so well is the way in which a child picks up and imitates the emotional habits of adults, especially of those adults she trusts and admires. It is almost a platitude to say that it is far more effective to *show* a child how to act than to *tell* a child how to act. But platitude or not, this is especially true in matters of emotional learning.

5. Dorothy Canfield Fisher, *Understood Betsy* (New York: Holt, Rinehart, and Winston, 1973), pp. 157–58.

Sometimes by imitation children explore new emotions that have not been part of their range of feelings before. Take as an example a family whose much-loved dog is struck by a car and killed. Families become very attached to pets, and it would not be unusual for some family members to have genuine grief over losing their loyal pet.

But grief over permanent loss is not part of the experience of many young children. It takes a degree of intellectual complexity for a child to understand the ultimacy of death and to imagine how it will be to walk into the house each day after school without the dog's wiggling welcome.

A school-age child who experiences some kind of permanent loss may have spontaneous grief—may sob, have a downcast face, and have drooping shoulders that express strongly her sense of hurt and sadness. However, a younger child may only be able to sense that something significant has happened, but be unable to comprehend exactly what. In such a situation it would not be unusual for a young child to try to gain a sense of the situation by imitating the emotions of others.

Sometimes emotional imitation is not entirely convincing, and it is clear that the grief is not heartfelt. But the expression is serious nonetheless; through imitation the child tries to get a feel for the emotions of others, and tries to clarify the situation emotionally in order to gain some grasp of its significance. Imitation and playacting are a child's form of empathy.

In a parallel fashion the emotions that children observe in others they may echo in play. Children use play in order to think things over, just as adults muse over events in order to assemble their own feelings and reactions toward them. Children do not have the intellectual control that adults have; they need props to help them stay on a topic and explore its possibilities.

By acting out a representative event through play, children sort out their reactions. Play is also children's way of empathizing, of reaching out to take in events they do not yet understand. Given the opportunity for some concrete experience, children show remarkable insight. Their inventiveness in staging events for reflection is quite ingenious.

Sometimes adults are amused by the caricatures that children make of adult behaviors when these behaviors are being acted out in play. Children who act angry in play are not actually angry. The play is in every sense an act put on by the child.

However, this should come as no surprise. Discussing anger and deepening our understanding of this phenomenon does not require that we be angry while we carry out this discussion. You do not need to be angry while reading this page in order to know to what it is that the word *anger* refers. Play, like reflection, allows some distance; however, it is distance based on experience. Very often children experiment with the examples adults provide them.

Emotional Partnership

Adults who are important in the lives of children are their emotional partners. Although children have strong emotions, and an amazing variety of emotions, their emotions are often less complex and less differentiated than those of adults. For this reason, an adult who has a genuine emotional attachment to a child may experience emotions vicariously on behalf of the child.

Take for example Susie's dad, who is sitting by the sidelines watching when Susie is up to bat in a ball game. The event may be quite intimidating for Susie, and for her dad as well. But Susie's dad may have a solid sense of confidence in her that is more elaborate than Susie's own inner sense of confidence.

As Susie stands at the plate waiting for the pitch, she glances over to her dad and sees displayed in his demeanor the confidence that she needs to face the challenge. Facing the situation alone, Susie might be overwhelmed by a threat of failure; but the confidence she feels through her dad becomes an extension of her own confidence, so that when the ball finally comes across the plate she has a sense of strength that she could not have had apart from her participation in her dad's feelings.

Vicarious emotion can also work negatively. If Susie doubts that she can hit the ball, and when she glances at her dad she sees that he doubts it, too, her dad's vicarious emotion may topple her fragile sense of confidence completely, so that she only makes a timid swing and completely misses the ball.

Sometimes the vicarious emotions that adults have for children are communicated only very indirectly. Davey may have very little sense that the street is a dangerous place. But, Mom and Dad, who vicariously experience the danger of the street for Davey, act in a way that provides protection for Davey that he could not provide for himself. We might go so far as to say that Mom and Dad are containers of the emotions that Davey is not yet capable of having, but that are important to his well-being nonetheless.

Let us take one more example. Sometimes in the play of children, one child is treated unfairly. It is not uncommon for schoolchildren to experiment with social power by forming cliques from which one child, for rather arbitrary reasons, is excluded. The same child who is excluded today may be included tomorrow and be just as vicious and unfair to a new victim as the other children are to her today.

The teacher who observes the unfair play of children may feel a genuine, vicarious anger at the injustice of these games, and may feel this anger even though the sorry little child who is excluded does not feel angry, but only feels hurt and bewildered.

The teacher feels anger empathically, and it is an anger for the sake of the victim. Thus, in a certain sense, the teacher's feelings are an extension of the victim's own feelings. This anger may even reach into a range of feeling that the victim, because of immaturity and lack of understanding, is not yet able to have for herself. That is why the partnership of an adult can help a child amplify useful feelings.

Earlier, when we discussed fitting emotion as one of the goals of emotional growth, we noted that one indication of an emotion's appropriateness is the action to which it leads. When a distressing emotion is fitting, it points the way to appropriate behavior—behavior that serves as a corrective and makes the distressing emotion no longer necessary.

When the playground victim only feels hurt and self-pity, her resulting behavior may provoke more nastiness on the part of the tormentors. But if she is provoked to a sense of righteous anger, it may unleash the strength that allows her to realize that this game of social manipulation is a silly and unfair game in which she wants no part. Such anger may give the child the courage to walk away from the game, and without a victim the game is over. The adult's vicarious anger, communicated in some way to the victim, may be just the extension of emotion that the child-victim needs in order to act appropriately.

Examples of emotional partnership between adults and children are infinite, but the above should suffice to make the point. There is, however, another important feature of this partnership that adults need to recognize if they are to make the partnership as effective as possible. While we serve children well in allowing their constructive emotions to be amplified through us, our service to them does not end with this. It is equally important that, where possible, we try to allow children to take back from us the emotions that we experience vicariously for them. We need to allow them to become guardians of these emotions for themselves. This step is essential to cultivating the child's healthy independence.

The balance between emotional dependence and independence is a fragile one. Adults are often uncertain as to how much they should involve themselves in children's emotions and at what point they should allow children to fend for themselves. Leaving children on their own when a supportive partnership is needed is neglectful, but involvement that is too aggressive may constitute interference. Adults who have ongoing emotional contact with children need to learn how to transfer to them the reins of the emotion they hold vicariously for the children.

Once again, an example illustrates the point. Remember Davey, whose protective parents are vicariously afraid of the street for him. If Davey's parents remain protective too long, he may not develop his own appropriate sense of fear. Thus, he may not become self-protecting, even at a point where he should know that while the street can be a dangerous place he can nevertheless navigate it safely with some caution.

When will Davey be able to take responsibility for crossing the street alone? When first he learns to be afraid of the street and then learns to master his fear with appropriate action. What is critical is the process by which Davey will take ownership of the fear. If he is maturing emotionally, he can learn to master his own fear. This is precisely what will happen when Davey's parents let him cross the street by himself because he is careful of traffic and looks both ways before crossing.

Sometimes it is difficult to hand over to children those feelings we hold in trust for them. This tension in the partnership of feeling is especially evident as children grow older, their wills become stronger, and we feel shame or regret for the poor judgment they use.

For example, Linda's mom discovers that Linda has submitted an assignment she copied from a classmate. She is ashamed for Linda, and perplexed that her daughter can be dishonest without feeling guilty. Linda's mom wants Linda to take over this vicarious feeling of guilt as her own, but regardless of how she tries to get Linda to be ashamed of her dishonesty, Linda will not assume this feeling. What should Linda's mother do?

The Gift of Guidance

When we notice how much children count on us to point the way to fitting feelings, we see how emotionally dependent children are. But when children resist assuming our feelings, we become equally conscious that our feelings are not theirs; they can also be emotionally independent of us.

The balance of dependence and independence requires critical decisions with regard to our emotional partnerships. We must decide when to persist and when to let go—when to allow children to follow their own feelings and bear the consequences.

Sometimes adults deliberately forge consequences. So for example, Linda's mom, after discovering that Linda has been dishonest about schoolwork, decides to inform the teacher of this dishonesty so that Linda will discover what happens in relationships in which good faith is sacrificed.

The intricate process by which children take over the feelings of adults has been carefully studied by developmental psychologists. They speculate that children first take over from their parents and later from other authority figures an image of themselves that embodies both an ideal of what a person ought to be and rules about what is not allowed and is thus worthy of guilt.[6]

Young children conform to the standards adults impose on them because they sense their dependence on adults. Little children do not dare to jeopardize an essential relationship by provoking disapproval or rejection.

Later, as children gain a sense of their independence, the influence of adults on them depends on their degree of identification with adults. Children who are bonded to adults by admiration and affection assume they are like the adults they admire. These children are willing to conform to the example of the adults.

In adolescence and adulthood ideal images and rules for behavior become part of the young person's own personality. Adolescents and young adults may have some ideals that differ sharply from those of their parents and some which are similar. But regardless of whether or not the young person's ideals are similar to or different from their parents', it is important for the young person to take ownership of them.

Psychological theories point out the legacy of our feelings. Every adult who takes on the responsibility of forming children was once also a child formed by powerful adults. This raises a very critical issue. Is the process of formation anything other than a blind process carried on from one generation to the next?

Adults who take seriously the responsibility of children's ethical formation must also take seriously the fact that there is more to an emotional partnership with children than the handing on of an uncritical legacy. The adult who wishes to be an effective guide for children must also be a self-critical adult. When we thoughtlessly pass to the following generation the habits a previous generation has thoughtlessly handed to us, the habits may become empty, and the legacy may become a burden.

The responsibility for ethical formation would be an overwhelming one apart from the confidence that there are sources of strength beyond us. The strength adults need is a spiritual

6. For an elaboration of this approach, see Robert R. Sears, L. Ray, and R. Alpert, *Identification and Child-Rearing* (Stanford University, 1965).

strength that allows them to be self-transcending. Religious faith is the source of this strength. The adult who is fit for a healthy partnership with children is one who trusts the promise of God's love and who understands that God's love is revealed in our love for our neighbor.

It is not only in the life of feeling and emotion that we share a partnership with children, but it is also in faith that we are their partners. It is neither possible nor healthy for us to construct in advance a formula for our own lives and the lives of our children. Living by faith requires that we *continually* stand ready to receive God's love so that, fortified by grace, we may act in good faith. A life lived by faith is full of surprises even while it is guided by a deep spiritual purpose.

Only if we can relinquish our own flawed habits can we be effective with children; and only if we can relinquish our own egocentric designs for children will we have the confidence to form them without feeling that we distort, possess, or manipulate them. In our lives our most sanctified goal is that God's image for us may take a unique and personal form in us—that we may become true persons with a strong center and firm relation to God.

The most sanctified goal we can have for the children we influence is that God's image may also be seen in them in a unique and distinctive way. Led by this goal, we can recognize that the responsibility of guidance is a gift, for we will believe that we are conduits of God's love for others. This is a high calling. It is a vocation in the truest sense. In accepting this vocation and its significance, we accept God's love both for us and for children. Assimilated into lives thus directed, our emotional partnerships with children become part of the ultimate partnership, a partnership with God through faith.

4

Emotional Echoes of Power and Attachment

In Chapter 1 we observed that emotional habits reflect personality. For example, some people seem to be jolly by nature, others are easily intimidated, and still others have hot tempers. Adults who form emotional partnerships with children become familiar with each child's distinctive pattern. Loyal emotional partners help children to understand, accept, and make the best of those patterns which are enduring traits in each child's character.

In addition to forming their distinctive emotional patterns, most children also go through predictable emotional phases. These phases are times during which children work especially hard at testing an important set of feelings about themselves. Children go through significant phases in learning to handle their needs for power and attachment. The emotions exhibited by children and those provoked in their parents during these stages deserve our special attention.

Strengthening Attachment

The attachments children form to their mothers have been carefully investigated by researchers. One of the important stages of this formation occurs in the first eight months of life. In most families it continues to be mothers who are infants' major care givers. However, there is good evidence that children can form strong bonds with any person who is a major source of comfort and affection during the critical stage for forming bonds.

In some unfortunate cases infants do not form solid bonds with adults. This is usually due to neglect or emotional disturbance on the part of the parents, or it can be due to tragic and unavoidable disruptions of the family situation. The consequences for children are considerable.

Children who suffer from attachment disorders, which is the technical way of describing the result of failure to form a satisfactory attachment during infancy, lack the basic ingredients for both social and emotional development. These children seem unwilling to look into the faces of other people, avoid making eye contact, do not adjust well socially, and do not respond normally to affection.[1]

Children who do establish an attachment to their mothers, or to some equally important adult, need to test that attachment now and again. They are like an old sailor who tests the anchor ropes before leaving the dock, because, he warns, "You don't want to wait 'til you're out in a storm before you wonder whether the cables will hold."

Children who test dependence are checking whether their attachments are strong enough to tolerate some tugs and pulls. This testing phase is usually quite short-lived. We must be clear here that we are not referring to children who are continuously dependent; that is a very different situation.

In my experience working with parents and children I have noticed that relatively short but sometimes intense stages of testing dependence often precede major leaps in development. For example, many babies go through a very dependent stage just before they learn to crawl.

One mother, who had been badgered by a clinging and whining child for several days on end, told me she felt as if her

---

1. See the *Diagnostic and Statistical Manual of Mental Disorders*, 3d ed. (Washington, D.C.: American Psychiatric Association, 1980) for a fuller description of this disorder.

baby had become a permanent growth on her hip. Her daughter wanted to be held constantly, didn't want her mother to leave the room, and would not accept any other care giver. A few weeks later, when I asked the same mother how she was getting along with her daughter, she smiled proudly and reported that her daughter had begun to crawl, and there was no keeping up with her.

Sometimes the shift from a phase of dependence to a phase of independence occurs within the span of a few days. When babies learn to crawl, or to walk, or to talk, the whole world takes on a new quality of adventure for them. Their energies pour into exploring this new world.

It is hard to know what goes on in a child's mind during a phase of dependence. It may be that children need to know how reliable adults are before they can muster the courage to go on to new adventures. This would not be particularly surprising. After all, adults go around taking leave of friends and relatives before they go off on adventures or begin long absences. Leavetaking is a way of solidifying bonds to which one hopes to return.

The process of testing dependence may occur at almost any time during childhood, but one very common time is just prior to when children begin school. The mothers of some preschoolers fret that they will never be able to get through the trauma of the first days of school.

The mothers of dependent preschoolers worry because their children follow them around, seem anxious when they leave, and do not want to venture very far afield from the protective range of their mothers' care. This is especially noticeable if it occurs in children who have already been more daring, sociable, and independent.

Fortunately for both mothers and preschoolers, the same child who seemed tied to Mom's apron strings can make a rapid shift to independence and become a confident school child. The child who makes the transition most easily is the one who has been reassured of its parent's support and dependability.

In school-age children tests of dependence may also be directed at teachers or other adults upon whom children have come to depend for security. Some children go through a dependency stage at the beginning of adolescence. Most adults expect power struggles during adolescence, but few are prepared for the feelings of helplessness, the inability to make decisions, and the deep confusion that is apparent in some children just before puberty.

The disorientation that is apparent in some pre-adolescents seems related to their sense that the old and familiar ways of childhood are slipping away from them, and they are overwhelmed by the prospect of growing up. At times it seems overwhelming for parents, too.

The specific form that a dependency phase takes depends on the child's age. But despite different ages at which they occur, dependency phases do have some emotional features in common. They are stages in which children tend to display their weaknesses as if to test how much adults are willing to fend for them.

Dependent children are quick to show distress in order to measure how much they can count on comfort. Old and immature behaviors may crop up in dependent children who need to check out how much adults will hold them to the progress they have already made.

Adults have their own emotional reactions to children who test dependency, and these reactions are, in many cases, mirror images of children's feelings. Adults tend to worry about whether children are losing ground or not matching up to other children their age. This echoes the fears of children who need to test whether adults will back them even in shaky times. Dependent children feel weary and overwhelmed; so do the adults who feel the full weight of a child's dependence.

Going through a dependency phase with a child often is not pleasant, but it is valuable nonetheless. Children who come out on the other side with a renewed sense of the loyalty and dependability of adults have gained a valuable asset. It is this goal that should guide adults in handling a child's dependency phase.

In exploring how to handle children's dependency it is helpful to separate behavioral components from emotional components of children's actions. In terms of their actual behavior, it is important to hold dependent children to the progress that they have already made in acquiring skills. For example, a child who has already learned to dress himself should not be allowed to set this skill aside to test whether his parents will step in and help him. Similarly, a child who has already learned to use cutlery should not be allowed to eat with her hands in order to get attention for acting helpless or babyish.

While it is important to help dependent children hold on to progress they have already made, it is not effective to counteract dependency by pushing children to develop new skills while they are going through a dependency phase. Parents can feel impatient with a child's bid for dependency and, in an effort to show that there is no choice about growing up, may put new demands on the child. Adults who push children during dependency phases may undermine their already shaky confidence and prolong the dependency.

In terms of achievement, a dependency phase is often actually a time of standstill. Fortunately, these phases are usually quite short-lived, and once children have accomplished what they need to in this stage, they go on to new stages of growth and achievement quite spontaneously.

But it is not enough for adults to deal only with a child's behavior during a dependency phase. This is a time when it is especially important for adults to also work along with children emotionally. Children in dependency phases need warm emotional contact. They need to know that adults can be reached, that adults will react affectionately to them, and that the connection is solid.

If children are too young for exchanging these assurances in language, then physical contact, warm smiles, and a kind tone of voice are especially important. A young child knows very well what is being communicated by a parent who spends comfort time with it in a rocking chair, or who laughs and smiles with it during a mealtime.

Even when children are old enough to communicate in language, the nonverbal expression of attachment remains important. But when language is included in the tools of communication it is important to talk with children about their needs for attachment. Children ought not to feel ashamed that they need to find security in adults, and adults should make that as clear as possible to children.

Let's consider an example. If a child during a dependency phase wakes up several times during the night and calls out for her parents, it is quite reasonable for one of them to say,

"I know it is very important to you that I be nearby. I will be. You can count on me. I won't go away without telling you. But I also need for you to be quiet during the night so that the rest of us can sleep. Even if you are quiet I will not forget about you or stop taking care of you."

The message of comfort to a frightened child is fortified by a quiet and reassuring voice. A hug or a kiss on the forehead tells the child that she is not rejected for feeling insecure. With this message the parent is accepting the child's need for reassurance on the emotional level and is giving some guidelines to the child for managing the need on the behavioral level.

Once adults open the door to communication and in a kind and accepting way acknowledge children's needs for security, children may talk more freely of their uncertain and uncomfortable feelings. Listening to them solidifies the attachment.

Many adults do not realize that promising to listen to the concerns of children does not mean that adults promise to solve any and every problem children present.[2] Adults sometimes try to rescue children where rescue is not even necessary. Children during dependency phases often present problems that either do not need to be or cannot be solved.

Let's look at another example. A child who is wakeful and needing his parents' assurance during the night complains that he is worried because someone told him that dogs live one year for every seven that humans live, and now he fears his dog will die sometime.

His parents cannot make the dog live forever, and they cannot assure the little boy he will not be bothered if something happens to the dog. Parents may feel stuck unless they realize that they do not need to solve this problem. It is sufficient for them to acknowledge that they, too, would feel sad if the dog died but would certainly be there to help their son with his sad feelings.

When children are testing their attachments they are looking for the reassurance that they will have emotional backing if they need it. Dependent children are not in a practical stage. The practical problems they present are very often actually set

2. For helpful advice about how to listen to children, see Thomas Gordan, *Parent Effectiveness Training* (New York: Peter H. Wyden, 1970).

up to test how adults will react to their emotional needs. Just being present and willing to listen is often enough to assure children that contact can be made.

It is always wise to thank children for disclosing their worries, even if you do not solve them. For example, the father who has listened to his son's worry about the dog might say, "Thank you for telling me what you are worried about. It feels good to me that you trust me enough to tell me about your feelings." That is a way of assuring a child that healthy attachment is as important to adults as it is to children.

Sometimes when adults are frustrated by the demands dependent children make, they attempt to stop the demands by threatening to take security away if children keep testing it. I recall being told by an adult that as a child he was once made to sleep in the basement because he was a poor sleeper and awakened his parents during the night.

Even as an adult this man could recall the terror he had felt alone in the basement, separated from the rest of his family. Threatening to make a child sleep in the basement may stop the child from calling out during the night to see if his parents are there, but it will not help to move him through the dependency stage. On the contrary, it may prolong it.

A child's dependency phase really tests adults; adult reaction to the pressure needs to be fitting. Adults are challenged to find ways of fortifying children's sense of security without being manipulated and controlled by them. In order to do so, adults must be able to distinguish themselves from the temporarily confused images children have of adults. At a minimum this means that adults must not take children's normal dependency stages as personal affronts.

The mother who assumes that her child is going through a dependency phase because of something she has done wrong in raising the child may try to compensate for past sins by letting her child control her. But a child who is already insecure will only feel more uncertain when saddled with the power to manage parents.

The father who takes the child's dependency as an attempt by the child to control him may withold reassurance as a way of showing the child who is in charge. This child will feel rejected, and rejection is no cure for dependency.

Parents of children in a dependency phase may have to deal sternly with themselves to avoid taking their children's dependency personally. Children's dependency, when it is a temporary phase, is not a consequence of parental failure. Admitting this is especially hard for parents who live in a culture in which it is believed that good children are always self-confident and capable, and that good parents keep them that way.

Most of us have to be average most of the time, because that is what average is by definition. But few of us are content with that. We like to think that we have a leading edge. Not only do we think that of ourselves; we also think that of our children. However, children who are going through a dependency stage are not likely to go along with the above average program, but not because they are trying to shame their families or make their parents look bad.

The dependency phases that children go through serve to illustrate a very important principle of emotional partnership. Adults cannot dictate children's feelings. Furthermore, children's feelings will not always be pleasant, and this is true of the most normal of children.

The test of a quality emotional partnership is not whether adults can make children act happy all the time. Any adult who tries to do this is probably not in touch with children's feelings, for the world is no more a perfect place for children than it is for adults. Sometimes unpleasant feelings are the most appropriate. Sometimes testing dependency is healthy.

Rather, the test of a healthy partnership is whether an adult can maintain solid emotional contact with a child so that together they keep moving along toward richness, fit and control of emotion. This may mean weathering hard times together, but hard times can be weathered well and with great benefit to both adults and children.

Testing Power

Lest we forget that attachment and dependence are just one side of a coin, we must move on to examine the other side, which is independence and power. Not only do children go through phases during which they test their dependence on adults, they also go through phases during which they test their independence. These phases, too, are a challenge to emotional partnership.

Children who are in a phase of independence are eager to explore what the limits of their control are; they are interested in their own powers to make things happen. Sometimes this curiosity takes very simple and benign forms. Billy wants to find out if he can hold his breath for a full minute. If he can, he puffs up his chest and feels proud. Susie wants to see if she can ride her bike with no hands. She feels like a big shot when she can.

Power testing is more complicated when it involves other people. If Susie is curious about whether she can persuade her little brother to go to the kitchen to get a cookie for her, and if she is determined to hassle him until he does, she is testing more than her own competence. She is testing her own power, her brother's power, and how the two mesh. Or if Susie decides to sell her bike to the neighbor kid for one dollar, she is testing the limits of her own decision making. She will need to find out what powers are hers to exercise, what powers are not hers, and what powers she may exercise only with her parents' permission.

Once again, we must be very clear that we are referring to a temporary phase in which children test independence. This assumes that children who are testing have already established solid emotional bonds with their parents. It also assumes that they have demonstrated, in earlier steps, the ability to be cooperative and compliant.

When we refer to children who are going through an independence phase of power testing, we are not including children who consistently and blatantly violate the rights and threaten the well-being of others.

There are children whose parents have been so negligent in setting standards or have been so arbitrary, harsh, or inconsistent in exercising power over their children, that these children do not understand what behavior is and is not to be tolerated. These severely disturbed children suffer from conduct disorders.[3]

Children who suffer from conduct disorders can be distin-

3. See the *Diagnostic and Statistical Manual of Mental Disorders*, 3rd ed. (Washington, D.C.: American Psychiatric Association, 1980).

guished from children who are merely testing power by both the extremity of the testing and by its duration. Children who are testing power operate at the border of what is and is not allowable. Children with conduct disorders tend to go farther out of bounds so that they violate widely held norms of acceptable behavior, and their violations tend to become more extreme over time.

It is a rule of thumb that the pattern of behavior that leads to the diagnosis of a conduct disorder must be of at least six months duration. A phase of normal power testing may go on for as little as a few weeks and is seldom of more than a few months duration.

The first encounter of many parents with power testing occurs when children are approximately two years old. Many two-year-olds go through a phase during which they check to see if their *no* works. Emotionally, a child's *no* sets up a tug-of-war. That allows a child to distinguish his will from that of his parents.

Parents who consistently give in to two-year-olds tell them in effect that they own their parents. That is more power than any two-year-old can handle. But the parent who harshly squelches the two-year-old's will is telling the child that he has no will of his own. Children who are thus taught can hardly be counted on to exercise their wills positively when the demand arises. What option is left to parents whose children test power?

Once again, it is helpful to distinguish the behavioral from the emotional component of a power struggle. When children challenge rules or threaten nonconformity, it is important for parents to hold firm behaviorally. Children should not be allowed to break rules just because they will be upset if they cannot have their own way, nor should they be allowed to break rules without consequences.

The *protest* of power-testing children is often the most difficult element for parents to accept. Most parents not only want compliant children, they also want children who are happy to comply. But this is more than a parent can ask during an independence phase.

While parents hold the line behaviorally, it is important that they do not engage in damaging emotional power struggles. Children do not need to feel humiliated, shamed, stupid, or powerless in order to know that their parents have authority; on the other hand, children do not have to like their parents' power in order to respect it.

Authority does not need to be arbitrary to demonstrate parental power. The best models of power for children are parents who are willing to give sufficient reason for demands.

Usually, sufficient reasons are those that state why the demand is in the best interest of both child and parent. But children do not have to be persuaded before they can be expected to conform. If good reasons have been given, parents have the right to expect *behavioral* conformity.

However, no parent can coerce *emotional* conformity. It is wise to listen to children's protests, and to acknowledge children's negative feelings. If it can be done without patronizing, it is helpful to reflect the behavioral and emotional levels back to the child once the child has complied with adult demands. For example, say, "I know you didn't feel like putting your bike in the garage, but I respect you for doing it anyway." Or "I know you don't think it was your turn to walk the dog, but thank you for cooperating."

Children who are focussed on their own independence are very sensitive to their parents' mistakes and very defensive about their own. This puts parents in a difficult bind. What do you do when you've made a mistake? What do you do when you've made a judgment based on faulty information, or there has been a misunderstanding due to an oversight or an error on your part?

On the one hand, it is very hard to admit weakness to someone who is testing your strength. On the other hand, the way you handle your mistakes serves as a model to your children as to how they should handle theirs.

Parents who make mistakes ought to admit them, but that does not mean that they forfeit all control in the situation. After acknowledging a mistake and apologizing, a parent may still expect to be treated with respect; and if there are further decisions to make, further limits to set, or further expectations to enforce, a parent still has the responsibility and legitimate authority to do so.

The power of forgiveness is one of the most important things parents can demonstrate to their children. In families children either learn how to forgive and to be forgiven, or they learn to shun this power. The example of parents is the decisive factor.

Parents who can forgive graciously show children that admitting an error revives strength. Parents who are able to ask for and accept forgiveness show that forgiveness is not a bitter pill that weakens those who take it, but rather that forgiveness strengthens people by strengthening their relationships.

A few months ago Jeanne and Richard were going through some power struggles with Mark. At their better moments they chuckled and remarked that Mark would make a terrific defense lawyer someday because there was nothing for which he couldn't think up an excuse. At their worst moments they were too frustrated to chuckle because Mark's flimsy excuses for the most obvious mistakes or misbehavior seemed so unreasonable.

One afternoon just before Richard arrived home there was a phone call for him, and in haste Jeanne scribbled down the message on a sheet of paper near the telephone. Unfortunately it was on the back of Mark's freshly finished math assignment. Jeanne's first reaction was defensive. She blamed Mark for leaving his homework lying about. No sooner were the words out of her mouth than she and Richard had to laugh. She might make a pretty good defense attorney herself.

Jeanne decided to bite the bullet and admit her mistake to Mark. She was pleasantly surprised that he smiled and said he didn't mind handing in a math assignment with a telephone message on the back. Jeanne and Richard were both aware that Mark was in a good mood at dinner, but they were truly surprised when he apologized because his glass left some messy-looking rings on his placemat. By this time Jeanne and Richard were feeling so good about Mark they hardly noticed that he was a messy eater. Jeanne's courage to admit her mistake gave Mark the strength to admit his.

The smaller the mistake the easier it is to admit it, but the bigger the mistake the more important it is to admit it. The courage to admit mistakes and be forgiven is not a very popular virtue. Standing up for oneself is more admired than backing down. However, the wisdom of forgiveness learned in childhood becomes a habit of the heart. It is a habit of the heart that also prepares us to accept the offer of divine forgiveness and grace. Children whose power struggles with parents teach them that admitting a mistake is a dead-end humiliation have difficulty believing that God's grace is not humiliating; consequently, their habit of refusing to ask and receive forgiveness robs them of spiritual power.

The styles in which children try their powers with parents change with age. The independence testing of school-age children is often exhibited in an exaggerated need for self-sufficiency. Homework is a favorite arena. It is irritating for children to discover that they have been asked to do something they are not *able* to do. Opening up the homework assignment and discovering that she cannot remember the instructions or cannot figure out how to do the task is a harsh challenge for the child who is in an independence phase.

It is no worder that parents are bewildered if they get an angry reaction to an offer of assistance with homework. No explanation is right. The first one you make is met by a reprimand that the explanation is not the way the teacher said to do it. If you ask how the teacher said to do the assignment, you are quickly shown how foolish your question is. "If I knew what the teacher said I'd be doing it, wouldn't I? That's why I asked you." In two seconds flat you know you are cornered; at least it seems that you are.

When a child is going through a phase of power testing it is very difficult for her to admit in one breath that she cannot do something and to admit in the next breath that someone else can. The independent child would much rather assert that she can do something that someone else cannot do, or at least that she can do anything anyone else can do. When she runs up against a difficulty, she feels pressed. If she can't do the task, she would rather that no one else can. This is not a rational struggle; it is an emotional struggle. It is wise for the parent to recognize it, but it is not wise to get caught in it.

The easiest solution for the child who feels incompetent at homework is to quit, but this is giving in to powerlessness. The parent who concedes to this solution allows the emotional level of the situation to overshadow the behavioral level. A more effective way of dealing with the struggle is to hold the line behaviorally while refusing to enter the emotional tug-of-war.

The child who sets up a no-win situation with homework

should be told, "I know you are frustrated and angry because your assignment is hard. I've felt that way myself sometimes, and it does not feel good. I won't help you with your homework this time because I don't think we can work together right now. You will have to do it the best you can. When you finish I want to see it, and you will have to explain to me how you did it. As long as you can explain to me how you did it we will not argue about whether it is correct."

An angry child may not welcome the parent's refusal to enter the fray. However, the adult who takes this approach brings the struggle back to a behavioral level. On the behavioral level it is reasonable to hold firm to the expectation that the child do the task as well as possible. At the same time, the best that can be done on the emotional level is for the parent to make the fairest and most honest statement he or she can, and leave it at that.

The most difficult stage of independence testing for most families is the one that occurs during adolescence. Adolescents establish their independence by demonstrating to adults that there are arenas of activity in which adult interference is not appreciated. Here are some examples. Adolescents have their own standards of fashion that distinguish them from adults, and adult opinions are considered irrelevent in this arena. Friendships represent a set of relationships distinct from the family. Privacy—private space in a household, private telephone conversations, and privacy to be with friends—becomes very important in adolescence.

The adolescent's ways of establishing independence make clear to both parent and child that their lives will become more separate as time goes on. The payoff of this separation is that it opens the way to genuine friendship between adult children and their parents. The ultimate goal is to reach the stage during which adult children and their parents share pieces of their lives with each other because they elect to do so and not because either of them can command it or because either of them cannot be self-sufficient without it.

The movement toward separate identities for parents and children involves a major turnover of control from parents to children during adolescence. Friction is created when parents and children are not moving at an equal pace. Parents want adolescents to take responsibility for things with which adolescents do not want to be burdened, such as household chores, schedules, and money management. And adolescents want to be in charge of matters over which adults are not ready to relinquish control, such as curfews, school performance, and social activities. It seems as if there is no agenda for the transfer of power that will satisfy both sides.

Parents of adolescents experience that their own power is being put to the test. It takes strength to stand up to disapproval while being honest enough to admit when there is confusion on both sides. Both parents and children have to make adjustments during the process of letting adolescent children become increasingly responsible for themselves.

In the final analysis, though, it is the responsibility of parents to monitor progress toward independence so that it goes on at a pace rapid enough to fortify the child's sense of power and not so rapid as to allow the child to become power drunk.

It helps parents to think in three-month spans and then ask these questions: "Does John have more freedom than he had three months ago? Where am I letting go? Is he taking some new responsibilities that he hadn't picked up yet three months ago? Where is he growing up?"

Being the parent of an adolescent requires the resolve to think in the long term while negotiating with a person who thinks in the short term. Sometimes that feels like an uphill battle. No doubt it feels that way to both sides.

Adults dealing with adolescents need to cultivate a tenacious belief that both sides can win and a refusal to believe that the contest can only be resolved with a winner and a loser. When children are made to keep household rules, to fulfill commitments, to meet responsibilities, to show respect for the well-being of others, they do not lose. They may not like it, but they are not weakened in the process.

When children are thrown into competition with their parents so that they have to take an emotional battering in order for the parent to gain the upper hand emotionally, children lose. They lose self-respect, they lose the ability to conform to expectations without shame, and in the long run they lose out on learning that the power contest can be brought to a fair solution through trust and cooperation.

Sometimes it is hard to keep sight of the balance of power while in the throes of a power contest. It is helpful as a parent, while having no intention of being controlled by your child at the moment, to promise yourself that, once you have established behavioral compliance, you will make a point of also affirming to your child some aspect of his power and independence.

Children need to know that they are respected, trusted, and admired when they use power well. Adults need to tell them.[4] Constructive accomplishments of handling power should not be passed over by being merely assumed and unmentioned. It is hard for adolescents to do things Mom and Dad's way. It is easier when they know that there are lots of things they can do their own way and that their parents admire them for that independence.

When an adolescent makes a good case for allowing an exception to a rule or for changing an agreement, it is wholesome for a parent to admit, "You've made a good case. I admire the way you've presented your view. I'm persuaded, and I'm prepared to go along with your plan." Such an affirmation of a child's power is made from a position of respect, not of intimidation. Acknowledging a child's constructive power rather than being intimidated by it is crucial for building trust and respect. Trust and respect empower both parties to make the exchange.

Dealing with power struggles is no fun either for children or their parents. But, it is a very important experiment for both of them. A child who never tests power may grow up more confused than a child who tests power and, in a healthy emotional partnership with a parent, learns the limits, the potential, and the fair sharing of it. The effort is well worth it.

Dealing with power struggles is not just a matter of solving problems. Power in a child is not a flaw. Parents who can form strength and independence in their children give their children a valuable legacy.

Christian parents sometimes ask whether children's testing of dependency or their struggles with power are not flaws.

4. For more on the developmental stages at which children learn to use power, see Erik Erikson, *Childhood and Society* (New York: W. W. Norton, 1963).

They wonder if the struggles are not signs that children, too, are sinners. I suppose behind their question is the assumption that if these phases are flaws, then they should be prohibited. But it seems that these parents are focussed only on the behavioral level and define sin as behavior.

Perhaps it is the case that perfect children in a perfect world would not have to test dependence, because they would have exactly what they needed and would never have to wonder whom they could count on. And maybe perfect children in a perfect world would not have power struggles. They would know their powers and always use them appropriately.

But talk about perfect children in a perfect world is quite beside the point. Those are not the normal children whom Christian parents are trying to raise. When children do not test power and do not test dependency in a way that gives them some clear sense of themselves and their relationships, they continue to test these matters well into adulthood. Adults who cannot get past childhood emotionally are more painful and tragic reminders of the world's imperfections than are children who work at childhood tasks in their appropriate season.

Adults who can work with children on the emotional tasks of childhood enjoy the growth of children, and they themselves experience profound reward. This is just one more way that the generations can stand by each other while dealing with the stuff of life. In this way they confirm the truth that we are not meant to be alone but are made to be in relationship with each other.

5

Emotional Growth and Sexual Development

In chapter 4 we saw how children's relationships with parents and trusted adults reflect both the children's ties to adults and their distinctiveness from them. The development of children's sexuality is also part of the constellation of their family relationships.

When we talk about the sexuality of children, we are not really talking about sex as the word is commonly used, which refers to bodily acts. Rather, childhood sexuality is woven together with the attitudes children have toward their own bodies and their need for human intimacy.

Because feelings about intimacy are learned by experience, not by instruction, there is no better place to develop them than in the family. The best sex education programs in schools, though able to provide information, cannot replace the satisfactory feelings that can best be cultivated in the wholesome atmosphere of lifelong relationships.

Even among adults who take the wholesome sexual development of children seriously, there are certain habitual forms of thinking that stand in the way. First, many adults incorrectly assume that sexuality in childhood is only important as

79

a preparation for adulthood, when persons become fully sexual beings. As a consequence of their future-oriented thinking, these well-meaning adults fail to realize that a child's sexual development is significant for that child's well-being in the present.

Second, many parents fail to take seriously the fact that sexual attitudes are primarily formed within the setting of family relationships. Their oversight results from their own ambivalent feelings about sexuality. They are uncomfortable with the idea that, because parental attitudes toward sexuality are handed along to children, they are significant partners in the development of their children's sexuality.

A Context for Understanding Sexuality

Each child begins life in a state of bodily union with his mother. Her body is the infant's world, and his body is enveloped by her womb. The mother's body nourishes the child, warms and comforts him, and protects him; the little one's lifeline is rooted in his mother.[1]

Birth is the first experience of separation. From this point onward the child's relationships with other persons—including relationships that are experienced bodily—take place within the fragile balance of connection and separation, of union and distinction.

Because we have come to think of sex as an act in which two separate adults come together physically, we have lost an appreciation for the fact that union is prior to separation, not separation prior to union. Recognizing the originality of union is important for parents who want to understand the sexuality of children.

In the first chapters of the Bible we find some very basic images of human relationship. The story of the creation of man and woman is a story about one person being brought forth from the body of another. It is a story of union prior to separation, and of separation making communion possible. First we are told that God says it is not good for the man to be alone, and then the story goes on to say:

1. For a helpful discussion of the role of mother and infant, see M. Esther Harding, *The Way of All Women* (San Francisco: Harper and Row, 1975).

So the Lord God caused the man to fall into a deep sleep; and while he was sleeping, he took one of the man's ribs and closed the place up with flesh. Then the Lord God made a woman from the rib he had taken out of the man, and he brought her to the man. The man said, "This is now bone of my bones and flesh of my flesh; she shall be called woman, for she was taken out of man." For this reason a man will leave his father and mother and be united to his wife, and they will become one flesh (Gen. 2:21–24).

One of the remarkable features of the biblical story is the image of a man giving birth. The story suggests that man and woman are as close to each other as a mother and the child to whom she gives birth. The story tells how two persons were formed out of one, and then how these persons who were separated from each other were joined together again.

Paul refers to this story and to the ongoing cycle of human relationships when he writes to the Corinthians, "In the Lord, however, woman is not independent of man, nor is man independent of woman. For as woman came from man, so also man is born of woman. But everything comes from God."

The continuing cycle of union issuing forth in separation and separation finding union again in communion weaves through the human race from generation to generation. It is repeated over and over as the physical joining of a man and a woman takes form in a child, who though tied to them forever by birth becomes a person distinct from them.

A description of sexuality in terms of the cycle of union and separation by no means implies that it is something ethereal or purely spiritual. Such a conclusion would flatly contradict the simplest human experiences that occur at various points in this cycle. The ongoing pattern is carried by and in our bodies. Sexual intercourse, childbirth, and the desire of vital persons to be connected to others may be mysterious, profound, and inexplicable events, but they are nonetheless bluntly bodily.[2]

Every child and every adult faces the challenge of realizing in the fullest and healthiest sense what it means that we are

2. For a helpful discussion of sexuality in the context of Christian values, see Lewis B. Smedes, *Sex for Christians* (Grand Rapids: Eerdmans, 1976).

bodily related to each other and bodily distinct from each other. This drama, which first begins to play itself out in the relationship of parents and child, is gradually extended to include others as well.

With the preceding remarks as our context, we can now turn to some of the most common concerns that adults have about the sexual behavior and development of children. These concerns often cluster around the following themes: the sexual development of children within their families, the role of sexuality in the relationships of children with other children, and the role of sexuality in children's feelings about their own bodies.

In each of these areas of sexual development children need guidance, and adequate guidance requires trust, respect, and skilled communication. These are all facets of the ongoing emotional partnership of children and adults.

The Development of Sexuality in the Family

Among the questions parents most frequently ask about sexual development are those dealing with standards of privacy and modesty in the family.

In the normal course of things, children are more physically intimate with their parents at birth than at any other time in their lives. In their most affectionate moments parent and infant conform their bodies to each other; the parent touches, strokes, and rocks the infant for the sheer pleasure of intimacy and affection. An infant nursing at his mother's breast is actually feeding on the secretions of her body. Such intimacy is made easy by children's lack of self-consciousness.

Not only is it easy for adults to be physically intimate with infants, it is also necessary. Infants deprived of warm human contact fail to thrive, even though provided with the necessities of nourishment, rest, and sanitary care. Infants need contact, and touch is the major means of such contact since words are not within the grasp of very little children.

Infants have no sense of modesty. Thus, they do not intentionally invade their parents' privacy nor do they know how to defend themselves against invasions of their own privacy.

If there are limits to be set, they are set by parents out of respect for the vulnerability of little children.

Things change with time. As children become more conscious of themselves they exercise more choice in the kinds of contacts they have with others. They are also more explicit in their demands for contact. For example, a child may ask to be held or to sit on a parent's lap, but this same child may not wish to hold her parent's hand in warm weather or be held too close when she is angry.

There are no hard and fast rules for what is or is not appropriate intimacy within the family. That is why developing a sense for what is appropriate based on wholesome feeling is terribly important. Parents can begin to make judgments about their own families and their own children by keeping in mind that habits of modesty within the family reflect the needs children and adults have for both intimacy and privacy.

Parents must also learn to be sensitive to the needs of each individual child, since not all children are alike. Some seem to have little need for bodily privacy, while for others it may be very crucial.

Especially when children are becoming conscious that they are keepers of their own bodies, they may ask for privacy. For example, it happens occasionally after children are toilet trained that they will ask to be left alone in the bathroom. Sometimes this is the beginning of a long-term habit, sometimes it is only a short-lived stage.

If children ask for privacy, their parents are wise to grant it out of respect for the child's needs for control. If children do not ask for privacy, it is not necessary for parents to impose it unless it is for the sake of their own comfort or that of other family members. Eventually, most children model their standards of privacy on the examples set by their parents.

The same balance of modesty should guide how free parents are with their children. If parents are at ease being observed while they are going to the bathroom, while bathing or showering, or while dressing, it is fine for them to be guided by their own feelings. Similarly, parents who are not comfortable with such exposure should feel free to be as modest as they wish.

Most children will absent themselves from situations in

which they themselves do not feel comfortable, but occasionally children will test the limits of their curiosity by silly comments or even embarrassed touching. If this happens repeatedly, parents need to help their child clarify the situation.

Parents may help embarrassed or teasing children by reflecting their uneasiness back to them. For example, a parent might say, "It doesn't feel comfortable when I dress in front of you." Such a comment clears the way for the child to express what it is that causes the discomfort. It may be that the child feels uncertain about, for example, why the parent's body is different from her own. Or, the child may be reacting to derogatory comments that she has heard elsewhere.

Sometimes children test the limits of their parents' privacy, hoping that some guideline will be set down for them. A child who pokes his mother's breast and laughs may be waiting to be told that aggressive or disrespectful touching is not acceptable. Parents and children need to discover together the comfortable balance of familiarity and distance for them.

Another concern that many parents have is what to tell their children about sexuality. One of the best signs of children's need for knowledge is their questions. Children often base their questions on their own guesses; the questions they ask are requests for affirmation or correction of ideas they already have. The best answers are both simple and truthful.

Consider, for example, the child who at the time his mother was expecting a baby asked his father if the baby would come out of Mommy's navel. His father gave him a simple and correct explanation, but the child looked worried. When his father asked him why he was concerned, the little boy wondered how his mother would manage that all by herself. When his father explained that someone would be there to help, the little boy was satisfied and went on to another topic.

Some parents answer children's questions with well-meant but confusing deceptions. We all know stories about babies coming from beneath cabbages or being delivered by storks. These stories not only delay the time for giving honest answers, but also shake a child's trust in parents as a source of reliable information.

Diversionary tactics subtly inject shame where it is not necessary, for children quickly catch on to the fact that parents do not mislead them about good news. Thus, if their parents cover the truth, it must be because the matter is either shameful or threatening.

Parents who answer children's questions with fictions seldom do so out of mean motives, however. They give evasive answers because they are caught without better answers and cannot think quickly enough to answer a child's question on a child's level.

It is helpful if parents, after answering one series of questions, give some thought to what the next series of questions might be. This gives them an opportunity to prethink how they will answer their children's questions most simply and directly.

A word of caution is in order for parents who do try to stay a step ahead of their children's questions. It is important not to run ahead of the questions when giving answers. A simple and direct answer does not need to be an elaborate lecture on sex education or physiology and anatomy.

The motive here is not to merely withhold information as long as possible; there is no good reason to withhold information from children when it concerns matters about which they have genuine curiosity and consequently are already thinking. Rather, children need time to assemble understanding. By going ahead of children's questions, parents run the risk of overloading children with information they cannot assimilate and thus of confusing them.

The principle of being guided by children's questions is not a moral principle but a pedagogical one. This same principle should operate when a child asks who puts up stop signs at corners. It is probably sufficient to tell a young child that workers come in a truck, dig a hole with a shovel, and put up the sign. If the child asks further about who tells the workers to do that, she might be told that a traffic engineer decides where signs are needed to help drivers, and then tells the workers where to put them.

It is overkill to give a young child an elaborate lecture on traffic ordinances, local and state government, and the adjudicative processes that come into operation when drivers go through stop signs. While all of that may be associated with traffic signs when an adult thinks about them, such a complex explanation goes beyond children's needs.

On the other hand, one of the easiest ways of educating children about bodily functions and sexuality is to not keep secrets from them in the first place. It was not long ago that children were intentionally kept in the dark about anything having to do with sexuality. What education they got they picked up from other children, by overhearing hushed conversations, or by happening onto books with suggestive covers.

Many children have suffered needless anxiety because of this sexual secrecy. Even parents who realized the folly of such secrecy and decided that they should tell their children "the facts of life" often found it difficult to do so after first hiding these facts for many years.

Many of today's mothers vividly remember the awkward encounters they had to endure as adolescents when finally mothers, teachers, or public health nurses decided the girls should be taught about menstruation. The embarrassment of such sessions was seldom due to the nature of the information itself, but rather to the fact that what was finally being told had already been treated as unspeakable.

Children from whom menstruation is not hidden learn about it very easily at an early age. When the eighteen-month-old child notices that men stand up while urinating, it is not a traumatic discovery. Similarly, children can learn that certain things happen to their mothers' bodies that don't happen to fathers' bodies.

If they ask about menstruation, they can be told simply that grown-up women's bodies produce some extra, unneeded blood and get rid of it. Most children are quite unimpressed by this; and as time goes along and more information is added to what these children already know, they accept it all as a matter of course.

A similar readiness to learn about what was once considered to be a strictly adult matter is manifest in the ease with which children accept the facts of childbirth when they are allowed to be present at home deliveries. Eyewitness experience is worth a thousand words.

Although there are benefits from direct experiences, there are also limits to the children's understanding of them. The most trustworthy indicators of the kinds of sexual matters that children are capable of understanding and accepting are their own expressions of comfort and discomfort. Because children frequently do not have words to label how they feel, it is important for parents to be attentive to the unspoken emotional cues that children give.

Parents who are alert to their children's feelings in all sorts of matters can learn to be skilled interpreters of facial expressions, body posture, and other gestures. The child whose face registers perplexity must be helped to search out and state the questions that need to be answered. The child who acts embarrassed must be helped to make clear what he finds awkward and unfitting. And most importantly, experiences from which children pull away are not appropriate for them. Parents should be alert to two emotional reactions in particular that may signal the limits to what a child can deal with regarding sexuality: jealousy and guilty secrecy.

When children begin to understand that their parents have a special sexual relationship with each other, they may feel confused. On the one hand, children have some curiosity and want to know about adult sex because they sense that it is interesting and important to adults. But when children realize that sex is a way in which their parents are intimate with each other and does not include them, they may feel left out and jealous.

It occasionally happens that children will object if their parents hug and kiss each other for no other reason than to show affection. While it is not necessary for parents to hide their affection for each other from their children, it is also not wise for parents to engage in intimacies in the presence of their children if their children cannot be included. The circle of a hug can be enlarged to include a child, but obviously, children cannot be included in their parents' lovemaking. The latter should be kept private from children. Parents are entitled to a life of their own; children shouldn't·have to be concerned with it.

When children ask questions about adult sex, they should be answered honestly, but in general terms. There is no reason for parents to share the details of their sexual relationship with their children. Because of this, the balance of discretion and disclosure become especially fragile as children near adolescence.

If parents do not remain open with their children, communication will stop. Parents can hardly expect their children to be personally open with them if they cannot be personally open with their children. What should parents do?

If children do ask personal questions of their parents, the questions are usually motivated not so much by curiosity about the parents as by the need children have to know about what they may expect for and of themselves. If parents wish to reciprocate their children's self-disclosure with personal disclosures of their own, they should share with their children the experiences they had when they were the age of their children.

Childhood experiences are the set of experiences that parents and children have in common. For example, to the child who admits feeling insecure in the locker room, the parent might recall those times he felt insecure about being in open showers because some classmates had better looking or more mature bodies.

The second emotional reaction that should signal caution to parents is guilty secrecy. Children may feel guilty if they believe they have witnessed something they ought not to have witnessed. Likewise, shame may be stirred up in a child whose own limits of privacy are transgressed.

The combination of shame and guilt is an important signal that a child is being made to deal with something that is more emotionally intense than she can manage with ease. For example, where intimacy or disclosure is too intense there is a strong impulse to cover it with secrecy. As a general rule, parents should not engage in intimacies with their children that they would not be able to tell a third party about, nor should children engage in intimacies with one parent if they cannot tell the other parent about it.

It is important here to distinguish between keeping secrets about acts and keeping confidences. There are times when children discuss matters with one parent that they would not feel comfortable discussing with the other. Such confidences should be kept out of respect for the privacy of children. Parents often do not realize how they embarrass their children when they lightheartedly entertain other adults by repeating what their children in all seriousness have confided to them.

While a parent ought not repeat the content of a conversation if the child has requested that it not be repeated, a parent would have no reason to keep secret the fact that he or she has had a conversation. Any parent should feel comfortable saying, "I had an interesting conversation with my child yesterday." But activities that parent or child cannot admit to a third party ought to be avoided.

Sexuality in Relation to Other Children

One of the ways that children learn about themselves sexually is by making comparisons with other children. In preschool children this takes the form of staring or unself-conscious touching. By the time children reach school age, however, they have learned that there are certain rules that guard people's privacy.

For example, what school-age child does not know that it is unacceptable to pull down another child's pants in order to see if that child's body looks like his own? Most children abide by these standards for behavior with remarkable consistency. It seems that they understand that such rules protect not only the privacy of others but their own as well.

In order to continue to satisfy their curiosity, school-age children construct games that allow them to break the rules for privacy in one sense while keeping them in another. These strategies take the form of sexual play. One of the most common ways in which children allow themselves to explore each other's bodies is a game called doctor.

Children know that doctors are persons who, though strangers, are allowed to look at those parts of their patients' bodies that are usually kept private from strangers. By playing the role of the doctor, the child casts herself into the category of an exception, as if to say, "Usually this is not allowed, but in this special case it is. When the game is over, it will not be allowed anymore."

Play is one of the means that children have for thinking things over. Just as an adult muses about something, children make it concrete and play it out. The strategy of acting out their reflections is also used by children to understand sexuality. Providing adequate supervision of children's sexual play requires special diplomacy on the part of parents.

Obviously, children do not want their parents to be involved in their sexual play, nor would that be appropriate. Nevertheless, the sexual play of children does require guidance from parents, just as does any other sort of play. When parents wink at the sexual play of children or pretend that it does not occur, they forfeit the opportunity to help children form healthy attitudes. In order to provide guidance, parents need to be clear about what is and is not healthy in children's sexual play. Once again, it is helpful to think in terms of a balance between intimacy and privacy.

There is no reason to assume that the dynamics evident in children's other play will not occur in their sexual play. In other kinds of play parents want children to show respect for their playmates, to control their aggression, to defend their own dignity, to be fair, and to show concern. When children slip into patterns that are mean toward or humiliating and demeaning of another child, parents try to help them see that there are unhappy consequences of such ways of dealing with others.

The same applies to children's sexual play. When parents discover that their children are involved in sexual play, they should respond by reminding their children to be good guardians of their own bodies and respectful of others'. This means children must clearly understand that sexual play is to be voluntary on the part of both children.

Children should not be made to reveal anything about their bodies that they do not choose to reveal. Younger children should understand that age does not give privilege or power, and older children should be made to understand that invading the privacy of younger children against their will or playing with younger children in ways they do not understand violates them.

Much of the sexual play of children is lighthearted and of little consequence, but this is not always so. There are adults who remember their first encounters with sexuality in childhood as being upsetting, humiliating, or shoddy, because they were at the mercy of an older child and did not feel they could appeal for help to an adult. And there are adults who also remember incidents in their own childhood behavior with a twinge of guilt, because from the retrospective glance of adult-hood they realize that they mistreated another child.

Inappropriate sexual play can be especially hurtful if it taints the memories of brothers and sisters. This need not happen if adults dare to be alert to children's sexual play, acknowledge children's curiosity, and help them in learning how to discern healthy from unhealthy forms of it. As a general rule, allowable sexual curiosity should occur between children who are the same age and stage of emotional development. Furthermore, an activity is probably not appropriate if it must be kept secret from parents.

Children and Their Bodies

We do not live in bodies; we are bodies. Knowing ourselves bodily is prerequisite to feeling at ease bodily. It is also pre-requisite to taking responsibility for how we live bodily with others. Of course, there are essential bodily functions about which we know very little. You may not know what keeps your heart beating or why your lungs fill with air, but you are con-fident, nonetheless, that they will. These are involuntary func-tions. Other bodily functions are under our control. They are voluntary functions. We may take speech as an example.

Infants much too young to speak make sounds with their voices, but speaking persons regulate these sounds and turn them into language. Language is, at least partly, voluntary. Now, the interesting thing about the control of speech is that, although we know how to speak, we do not know all of the details of what we do in order to speak. Likewise, when we refer to knowledge of bodily functions, we need to have at least two sorts of knowledge in mind: knowing how and knowing what.

"Knowing how" comes from experience, and results in the ability to control an action or function. "Knowing what" comes from thinking, and produces ideas about an action or function, although knowing about something does not necessarily imply ability to control it. For example, a linguist may know about and be able to describe the difference of the French *r* sound from the English *r* but be unable to produce both sounds in his own speech.

Distinguishing between voluntary and involuntary functions, as well as between knowledge of how to do something and knowledge of what it is, is important for our understanding of what children learn as their sexuality takes form.

Many of the functions that are involuntary early in life become voluntary as children mature. For example, male babies have erections that are purely involuntary, but adult males have at least some control over this same function. In order for involuntary functions to come under voluntary control, some kind of learning needs to take place. Unfortunately, the failure to distinguish "knowing how" from "knowing what" sexual responses occur in the human body has resulted in some unrealistic views of how children learn about themselves sexually.

Many adults, convinced that children need to know about sex, look for just the right book, filmstrip, or sex education curriculum for introducing children to knowledge of the human body. They assume that the right labels, drawings, and ideas are what children need. These same adults hedge considerably at the suggestion that children also need to know their own bodies, and that from experience they gain knowledge of how their bodies behave since they are their own most vivid exhibit.

In the case of bodily functions and sexual feelings it is important for children to know how their bodies function, because "knowing how" is personal knowledge that allows not only for familiarity but also for control. And control is essential in the exercise of responsibility. Once children know how their bodies behave they may also seek out more general knowledge as a way of assuring themselves that they are normal and that what is true of them is true of others as well. Feeling normal is important for a sense of comfort and ease.

Most adults, when asked if they explored their bodies when they were young, will admit that they did. There is every reason to believe that children always have been and always will continue to be curious about their bodies—that they will look at themselves in order to form images of their bodies, that they will touch themselves to discover how it feels, and that they will experiment with their bodies to make interesting things happen. But most persons who remember their own childhood explorations also recall that adults did not approve of them.

Adults have some subtle and some not-so-subtle ways of discouraging children from being interested in their own bodies. Children may be told that they should not put their hands inside their clothing, that touching some parts of their bodies is dirty, that "nice" children do not play with themselves, or that masturbation is addictive. Having encountered such adult disapproval, children have two options: They can become furtive about their explorations or they can discontinue them. Both of these options deserve our scrutiny.

Children who continue to explore their bodies in spite of adult disapproval do so with a certain amount of shame. They are likely to conclude that these functions, even though interesting and pleasurable, are built-in weaknesses or causes of sin. Furthermore, the sexuality they feel uneasy about in themselves they may also demean in others. One common way in which this crops up, for example, is in the assaultive humor of adolescents, the point of which is to ridicule someone else for something sexual.

Children who discontinue their sexual explorations and succeed in stifling their sexual interests may remain ignorant, but they remain sexual beings nonetheless. Children and adolescents who do not know how their bodies work may feel frightened about being sexually inadequate or anxious about being overwhelmed by their sexual feelings.

Persons who feel incapable of managing their sexuality also have difficulty taking responsibility for it once it does come to expression. For example, the irresponsible sexual behavior of some promiscuous girls that results in damaged feelings and sometimes damaged futures often has behind it enormous feelings of helplessness and a refusal to take their sexuality seriously.

Therefore, both hiding and stifling sexual exploration may have undesirable consequences. More immediately, the pressures to do so may make children feel uncomfortable about their bodies; in the long term, suppressing their sexual exploration may leave them unprepared to take control of and responsibility for their own sexuality and for the relationships in which sexuality takes on a special importance.

However, adults should not push children to be sexual nor amplify the importance of sexuality for them. For the most part, adults are wise to leave children at peace with their explorations, and when the explorations become apparent to simply acknowledge them as normal and private. This acknowledgment, and even permission, communicates to children that their sexuality is a good part of life and that it is worthwhile to be a good guardian of it.

Giving children permission to be interested in themselves sexually is not a license to immorality. On the contrary, such permission demonstrates the practical value of advice that parents give to children. For it makes little sense to tell children that they should ignore their bodies as much as possible and that when they cannot they should break the rules only a little bit. Rather, children need to be told that they may enjoy their bodies if they become good guardians of them. And children need to be taught that intimacy is good, but only when built on healthy attitudes and respect for others. By helping children form healthy attitudes toward themselves and toward others, parents can help their children become truly ethical persons—also sexually.

6

Other People's Children

The ways parents interact with children and the ways children interact with other adults are different enough to be obvious to almost any observer. And it isn't surprising that the contributions parents and other adults make to the development of children are quite distinct.

Parents who entrust their children to the influence of other adults need some sense of the special qualities of these relationships. Similarly, other adults need to understand that they are neither expected to be duplicate parents nor to compete with them. With that in mind, let's consider how adult friends and relatives differ from parents, and then consider the special contributions they can make to children's emotional growth.

I find it helpful to think of the relationships of children with adult friends and relatives as auxiliary relationships. We must be clear that we are not referring here to grandparents, relatives, or foster parents who have primary responsibility for children, nor are we including adults who live with children in the same household. Rather, auxiliary adults have intermittent contact with children, and the bond between them is based more on affection than on responsibility.

A while back I was at a restaurant for lunch and, as luck would have it, seated at a table next to a distraught little boy

who couldn't have been more than four years old. This little
fellow did not want to eat what his mother had ordered for
him, but he wanted to eat something, and he had her going in
circles in a futile effort to keep him quiet.

Mom gulped down her own food and left in a hurry. There
is a certain angle to the arm and a certain fall of the foot that
marks a child who is being towed to a more private spot where
the real confrontation will take place. His arm definitely had
that angle, and his gait had that distinct "to the gallows" quality. I felt sorry for both of them. All children have these moments, and they are difficult.

A few days later I happened once again to be at a table next
to a preschooler. This little fellow was with his grandparents,
and they were having a great time. He couldn't have been on
better behavior, but frankly his grandparents couldn't have
been better, either. He was enthusiastic and charming, and his
grandparents were there to admire every wrinkle of his nose,
every word he spoke, and every bite he ate. This is the "other
people's kids" phenomenon.

More than once I have heard grandparents comment that
they enjoy their grandchildren more than they were ever able
to enjoy their children. It's not that they love their grandchildren more, but being grandparents seems easier. Grandparents
can chuckle about spoiling their grandchildren without really
worrying that they are ruining them. This luxury is not peculiar to grandparents. The adult friends of children seem to
enjoy this same privilege. There is something distinctive about
these relationships. What is it?

The Luxury of Simplicity

The lightheartedness of auxiliary relationships is due in part
to their simplicity. Auxiliary adults do not have to plan for
children's futures; they do not have to be conscious of over-
seeing all the various arenas of children's lives, and they do
not have to take major responsibility for forming children's
habits.

The extent of a parent's responsibility is part of what makes
being a parent seem weighty at times. Auxiliary adults are
allowed to be much more momentary, much more focussed on

a single event, and much more tolerant of children's habits. In short, they are allowed to be much more child centered.

When Grandmother bakes cookies with her grandchildren it is done for the sake of childish inventiveness; the goal is not to produce cookies that can win a 4-H prize. Anyone who bakes with children needs to understand that usual standards of tidiness are not likely to be met. Children spill flour, and they are not experts at spacing cookies on the cookie sheet. But it doesn't matter if the intent is to have child-centered fun.

Children flourish in child-centered circumstances that give them the undivided attention of adults. When adults express their affirmation of children in a very condensed way, the children feel very admired and important. Children's feelings of pride and self-confidence are bolstered through this experience. No wonder such events seem so special.

Perhaps parents can learn from the example of auxiliary adults. It should be possible for parents to set aside their elaborate concerns and be child centered now and then. But doing so requires creating the mood of an event. It means allowing an event to be enjoyed for its own sake from a child's point of view.

Those golden times when parents are child centered sometimes require setting aside usual standards for behavior. I am reminded of an acquaintance of mine who recently spent an entire day sewing doll clothes with her daughter. Normally, this little girl is not allowed to use the sewing machine, but on this special day she was.

A difference between the child-centered attention of parents and of auxiliary adults is that parent-child relationships are not as simple as auxiliary relationships. Children need to experience the child-centered attention of their parents, but parents cannot always be child centered.[1]

One of the challenges that children grapple with is learning that sometimes it is necessary to relinquish the attention they so much crave while trusting that when it is necessary they will gain back the attention they need. It is a difficult task. At

1. For a view of development which balances children's needs and parents' interests, see Erik Erikson, *Childhood and Society* (New York: W. W. Norton, 1963).

times in their own families children need to relinquish the focus of attention in the interests of practicality. Even more difficult for some children is the need to relinquish attention so that someone else may have it.

When my little friend spent a day sewing with her mother, she also had to adjust to the fact that the next day it was back to business as usual. Parents have to face the challenge of finding a way to balance child-centered events with all of the many events that need to be attended to in a household. For auxiliary adults it is simpler; when the times of concentrated attention are over they send the children home.

Once again we must add a qualification. Just because an event is not child centered does not mean that it is at a child's expense. Consider this example. When Jennifer helps her dad carry the trash containers to the curb for pickup, she is not participating in a child-centered event. It is not realistic to think that they are doing this task together for the fun of it. At the point Jennifer decides the activity really isn't much fun because the containers are heavy and smelly, she is not free to walk away. Because the task has a practical goal, it is Jennifer's responsibility whether it is fun or not.

Even though carrying out the trash is not a child-centered event, it is good for Jennifer. She is proud of herself for carrying out this task well, and she senses that she is really helpful. Working along with her dad is good for Jennifer if it gives her a feeling of comaraderie and the experience of cooperation.

It is extreme to say that children's relationships with auxiliary adults are entirely child centered while their relationships with their parents are not. However, the proportion is different. Auxiliary adults make *fewer* demands on children, and because there are fewer tasks and obligations to mesh with auxiliary relationships, they are simpler.

Voluntary Relationships

Long ago, in a source I cannot even remember, I was stunned by an author's observation that sooner or later every child is hard to like. There are times when the most devoted parents are pressed to love their children, even though they don't like them. Loving in this case means sticking with children, not deserting them or giving up on them when they are nasty, difficult, trying, and disappointing.

Hopefully, it isn't often that a parent's love is tested by a child who for the time being is not likable. But it is only realistic to recognize that in every parent-child relationship this does happen now and then.

Lest we place all of the responsibility on one side, we should recognize that parents are not always likable, either. Children do not choose their parents, nor can they select another set if they discover that they do not like the ones they have. In those very exceptional cases in which children are removed from the care of their parents, it is not because the children do not like their parents; it is because the relationship is so inadequate that the children's health, well-being, or even survival are at risk.

One of the important skills that children learn in families is emotional endurance. In a peculiar way it is reassuring for children to learn that relationships survive tough times. This is what happened when Jeff left his bike in the driveway once again after being cautioned that if he did so he would not be allowed to use it for a week.

When Jeff's mother put the bike on dry dock, Jeff was angry. He sulked and scowled at her every chance he had. Clearly he didn't like her, but she was still his mother. And as we might expect, once Jeff got over the conflict with his mother, their relationship was just as good as it had been before. Maybe it was even better, because it had been put to the test and shown to be durable.

Auxiliary relationships normally need not endure the tests that parent-child relationships do. The hard work of child rearing is left to parents, and auxiliary adults understand that they do not have to take on the heavy responsibilities that parents do. Children also seem to sense this. They do not test auxiliary relationships in the same way that they test their relationships with parents.

Because difficult times and stressful interactions can be held to a minimum in auxiliary relationships there is a tendency to idealize them. They are pleasant relationships. Children thrive in them, but children could not survive emotionally with *only* these relationships. They also need durable relationships that can survive unpleasant times. When we consider the total picture, there seems to be a trade-off operating. Parent-child relationships are complex but durable. Auxiliary relationships are simpler but more tentative.

Having compared parent-child relationships with auxiliary relationships we can move on to consider some of the special contributions that auxiliary relationships can make to children's development. Among the many benefits of auxiliary relationships three are especially supportive of children's emotional development.

Trying New Images

Children change a lot as they grow up, and sometimes the changes are quite dramatic. But changes are not always easy for them to make, even when they are changes for the better. Roles and relationships are habitual. When we deal with each other every day and in routine ways, we get into patterns that have a momentum all their own. Changing those patterns takes attention and adjustments, and that may translate into resistance to change.[2]

Built into familiar patterns of children's interactions with their parents is a resistance to change. So, when children are ready to change their emotional patterns, they must overcome that resistance. If the changes they are considering are still tentative, they may not have enough force to overcome that resistance. But with an auxiliary adult whose way of interacting with a child is not set into a strong and familiar pattern, the child may find it easier to make the change. It is in part for this reason that children often seem to be older or on their best behavior when interacting with auxiliary adults.

In fresh circumstances children are free to try out their most grown-up images without drawing attention to themselves or surprising anyone. Furthermore, trying out those best images is not nearly so committal as it would be if it were tried at home. Interaction with the auxiliary adult is temporary; it doesn't set patterns for the long term. But at home it is much

---

2. For a discussion of how children develop and understand their social roles, see R. C. Ziller, *The Social Self* (New York: Pergamon, 1973).

harder for children to go back on new accomplishments once they have demonstrated that they are capable of new levels of competence.

Melanie stayed with friends for three days while her parents were out of town at a wedding. When her parents returned to pick her up they were profuse with their thanks, but her hosts played it down by emphasizing how self-sufficient their little guest had been.

Melanie's hosts praised her for getting herself ready for school in the morning: dressing, brushing her teeth, combing her hair, and doing all of these things without needing to be reminded. Her parents were amazed. These were routines with which Melanie required help at home, or at least ample reminders.

How many parents have not had a similar experience? Children go away to camp for a week and when they come back they seem a year older. Or, the parents of your child's friend remark how extremely well-behaved your child is, while you have that same impression of their child when he is at your home. When children are away they are often on their best behavior because they are free to try out their very best images of themselves.

Discovering Diversity

Experiencing variety is good for children. Learning to operate in different arenas develops flexibility, and this flexibility in turn shores up confidence. Children who have had some variety of experience dealing with auxiliary adults are not as fearful as they would otherwise be when faced with something new. They know that they have faced the unfamiliar before and done well with it, so in all likelihood they can handle the unfamiliar again.

It is the privilege and responsibility of parents to decide what diversity falls within an acceptable range and what goes beyond tolerable limits. When Stacey stayed at her aunt's house, she was not allowed to take snacks into the living room. At home Stacey is permitted to take snacks anywhere in the house as long as she brings the plate or the glass back to the kitchen and does not leave litter. Different households have differ-

ent rules. Stacey had to learn which rules apply in which
households.

There is another situation that came up when Stacey visited
her aunt. In that neighborhood there is a handicapped child
who has slurred speech and a lurching gait. Some of the children in the neighborhood ridicule this handicapped youngster.
Whether Stacey's aunt will tolerate it or not, Stacey's parents
do not want Stacey to do this when she visits her aunt's home.
If it is a matter of principle with them they should be free to
ask that when Stacey is away from home she be helped to
observe the same standards of respect for others that she has
been taught at home.

When parents help their children sort out the diversity of
habits, rules, and values that come into play in their interactions with auxiliary adults, a valuable form of learning is taking place. Children learn that various standards have varying
priorities. There is a difference between a rule that is a matter
of convenience and one that is a matter of ethical principle.
An arrangement for today is a standard of one sort, but a moral
requirement is another matter.[3]

Christian parents who are concerned with how they can
raise children of conscience and how they can instill Christian
values would do well to consider how adults outside the family
serve in this process. Many of the values children learn they
learn within the family. However, they also learn a great deal
about the role their family plays in a community of some sort.

Adults with whom children form relationships represent the
extension of the family into the community. By community I
do not mean a neighborhood or a geographical locale; rather,
I mean a group with which a family feels a lasting affinity and
with which it can identify a common purpose. Children get to
know their parents by the company they keep. Children get to
know their parents even better if they get to know their parents' company personally. Experiencing diversity within the
community of faith and commitment is healthy for children.

Where a sense of community is broken, living with diversity

---

3. For a survey of theories about moral growth, see Eleanor Maccoby,
Social Development: Psychological Growth and the Parent-Child Relationship
(New York: Harcourt Brace Jovanovich, 1980), pp. 295-364.

can be very difficult for children. This is the predicament of many children whose parents are divorced. Custody arrangements often require that children move back and forth between two households, and the system of expectations established by one parent rarely matches exactly that established by the other parent. Differences can become a battleground, and children can be injured in the crossfire.

There is no simple solution for the tensions that occur with divorce, but understanding the role of auxiliary adults may encourage some creative thinking. The healthiest solutions are those which take into consideration the best interests of children and *both* of their parents, even though divorced parents may be angry with and feel slighted by each other.

It is helpful if a divorced parent evaluates what falls within and what falls outside of a tolerable range of diversity. Divorced parents who carry out this exploration may find that they can tolerate hardly any diversity with each other. All differences are painful reminders of their own incompatibility. As far as children go, however, it is reasonable for divorced parents to work toward tolerating in each other the same range of difference that they tolerate with relatives, friends, or grandparents. In other words, although parents are not really auxiliary adults, it may help divorced parents to think of each other that way. Then when they evaluate diversity they will have the graciousness to recognize that unless the discrepancies are quite important, it is best to let them go and trust that children can learn that different households have different expectations.

The most difficult situations for a divorced parent arise when an expartner's handling of a child violates moral or ethical principles that the parent holds dear. The helplessness a divorced parent feels in this situation is enormous, and it is especially hurtful because it involves something as precious as a child. If the violations involve abuse, neglect, illegal acts, or baldly antisocial behavior, legal intervention is necessary. But, short of those extremes a concerned parent's best recourse is a persuasive appeal to the child.

Although difficult, it is sometimes very effective for a divorced parent to assume the attitude of an auxiliary adult in helping a child deal with the other parent. A helpful auxiliary adult listens to a child's feelings toward and observations of a parent, but is cautious about imposing his or her own views of the parent on the child. Children should not be expected to mediate the complaints adults have about each other.

A helpful auxiliary adult encourages a child's strength and virtue in dealing with a parent, but it is not helpful for an auxiliary adult to feed a child's resentment toward a parent. Children have little choice about the parents they have, and resentment does not encourage a child to engage a parent in constructive communication. For example, it is more helpful to encourage a child to explore ways of approaching a parent to talk than to malign the parent by predicting that he or she will not be willing to deal with the issue.

In my experience with children of divorced parents I have almost never found that a parent can strengthen his or her own efforts to train a child's behavior or attitudes by convincing the child that the other parent is bad or wrong. Parents also need not idealize each other for children, because children are quite skilled at drawing their own conclusions from experience.

Along this same line I have observed that the most constructive parent is the one who is willing to listen to a child's concerns without needing to interrupt to correct or indoctrinate; is fair and flexible in dealing with conflicts he or she has with the child; and is morally and ethically courageous enough to present his or her own ideals to the child and is humble enough to admit to the child that living up to these ideals is not always easy. In other words, it is a rough rule of thumb that a divorced parent's energies are better invested in maintaining the quality of time spent with the child than supervising time spent with the other parent. It isn't easy to let go, but fortified by conviction and the love of their children, divorced parents can take up this challenge.

The Luxury of Having a Good Listener

Auxiliary adults make good listeners. They have some distance that lets them listen without prejudice. Counselors, for example, are auxiliary adults. I am often struck when I do therapy with children that the most valuable time we spend together revolves around times they trust me to be a good listener. It is when they give me a chance to listen that I get to know the children with whom I am dealing.

It is important for parents to listen to children, too. The most frequent complaint that adolescents lodge against their parents is that parents do not listen. Probably these parents seem not to listen because they are too eager to correct what their children think and say. If listening were just a matter of hearing and all it required is getting within earshot and letting the sound waves of a child's voice strike the ear, I suppose most parents would have little difficulty with it. For example, most parents have no difficulty overhearing their children arguing with each other. Hearing and listening are not the same.

There is something very important involved in the difficulty parents have listening to their children when parents are afraid of what they will hear. Lynne, who is a particularly eloquent young lady, described her father's inability to listen this way: "The moment I say something to my father, it feels like I've pushed the button on a tape deck and I get a prerecorded sermon."

Lynne's father was not an unloving father, but he was very anxious about getting Lynne to behave as he wanted. He didn't dare listen to her, because he did not realize that the respect he showed Lynne by listening to what she had to say would be reflected back in the respect Lynne showed him by listening to what he had to say. Conversely, the disrespect Lynne's dad showed her by turning a deaf ear was the counterpart of Lynne's disrespect for his sermons.

Auxiliary adults have an easier time listening, partly because they do not feel responsible for getting children to behave as they are supposed to behave. So auxiliary adults take it easy and listen. Listening is respectful, and children end up listening to auxiliary adults in turn. This makes them powerful people in ways they may not intend or even realize.

Often when dealing with children who have behavioral problems, I have been amused at how easy they are to deal with in my office. When I was first learning to do therapy I sometimes entertained the fantasy that if I could take a troubled child home we would get along just fine. After all, I understood the child, and we got along so well in my office.

Over time I have come to realize that I could not be a heroic parent to the children with whom I do therapy. At home I would have to remind these children about bedtime, supervise homework, be the nasty mother who serves liver instead of pizza at dinner, supervise play with other children, and still find time for myself. Listening would take on a different character then, and my heroic image would tarnish very quickly.

By recognizing that at times it is not easy for parents to listen to their children, I do not wish to suggest that parents are excused from the responsibility of listening. Parents need to know their children if they are to deal with them effectively, and there is no other way to get acquainted than by communicating.

We need, however, to dispel the myth that listening is easy for parents and that parents who fail to listen are denying their children something that would take no effort at all. Rather, we need to understand that listening may be very hard work, but it is worth it. Parents who want to be better listeners might get some helpful hints by observing how auxiliary adults do it.

The kind of listening that auxiliary adults do is "free" listening. It involves just letting a child talk, with the understanding that the adult is not intending to fix up, discredit, or judge what the child has to say. This is child-centered talk.

Parents can't always be child centered. We reflected on that earlier when we considered child-centered events. But now and then, and the more regularly the better, parents need to indicate to their children that they are ready for some child-centered talk.

Talking has an important emotional function. In talking about an event, feelings about it are clarified. I have frequently had college students visit my office to ask a thirty-seconds question about my lecture and then stay a half hour longer to talk about their families. They weren't there to solve problems, or complain, or even ask questions. They were there to reflect, and talking to someone helped them reflect. Talking about their families for a few minutes was for these college students a way of going home for a few minutes. And I was privileged to accompany them on their visits. It was also their way of letting me get to know them, by letting me get to know about something important to them.

It is a very wonderful thing that people can learn about themselves by telling their own stories. This is just as true of children as it is of adults. By telling their stories they get a better hold on reality, and even if it isn't exactly the way they would wish it to be, having a hold on it feels better.

Parents should never overestimate how well they know their children. Free listening always adds something new. Free listening is also one of the ways that people who love each other show that they like each other.

At one time I worked with a school-age girl, Caroline, whose preschool brother was profoundly deaf. The family was determined to give her little brother every possible assistance they could. He was making good progress. Caroline was very loyal to her brother, but she needed to tell straight out what it was like for her to live in a family where another child needed so much attention.

As Caroline told her story, she seemed to smile more and more. It was clear to me that she did not expect me to help her brother, or to take the work away from her family, or even to convince her not to care so much about the hardship that had come her way. She just needed someone to hear her story on her terms.

Caroline could not talk with her parents the way she talked with me. They could not have kept their own stories separate from hers. I could. I was not part of her family. I was a listener. Furthermore, Caroline's parents were very devoted parents, and they would have wanted to do something for her. That kind of invested listening is not the same as free listening.

The role of auxiliary adults in the lives of children serves as a good reminder that no one owns children. Friends, relatives, parents and others are partners and guardians who share in children's lives. None of these relationships serves children well if it becomes so possessive that it excludes others. But all of these relationships in their own ways encourage children to extend the reaches of their experience to include others.

In some traditions children have godparents. Over the years the role of the godparent has become quite diminished and its use is no longer clear. Godparents are considered more exotic than necessary. It is interesting that godparents were at one time meant to be auxiliary adults. They actually took vows to assume a very special guardianship for their godchildren.

Perhaps the time has come to revive the tradition. What a very special gift it would be for a child to have a committed auxiliary adult following along the course of its life from birth. The parents who invite such a relationship open the door to the resources of relationships outside of the family. But whether or not the designation is godparent, the adult who enters such a relationship offers a child a very special human gift.

7

Teachers and School

In chapter 6 we reflected on those special relationships that help children reach beyond their families. Teachers are also part of that group of adults who influence the emotional development of children beyond the range of home life. But teachers are unlike other auxiliary adults in that their relationships with children are not simple. Following are some important differences.

Children at school must learn to share the focus of attention with other children. Consequently, they are even less the center of attention at school than they are at home. The adult who coordinates the activities of many children at once has the role of a diplomat. It is a role quite distinct from those of parents and of auxiliary adults.

It is also significant that children's relationships are involuntary. For a block of time the relationship is obligatory and intensive; nevertheless, it is temporary.

School-age children move through a series of relationships which require that at the beginning of each school year they adjust to the influence of a new adult and at the end they let go of the attachment. Adults may underestimate the loss that children feel if their relationships with teachers have been trusting and happy.

The role of teachers with children is task oriented. Teachers do not choose to spend time with particular children because of a natural attachment or because of special affection. Contact with children is teachers' work. Furthermore, children's contacts with teachers are also task oriented. The teacher directs children through tasks that are governed by standards of accomplishment and that require discipline. School is children's work.

For understanding the emotional development of children at school, I find it helpful to think of the teacher as a task mediator.[1] Although children's relationships with teachers are very important, there are other features of the school setting that are equally important.

Some reflection on the way the school environment influences the emotional development of children is merited for several reasons. First, children spend a large portion of their first eighteen years in school. The sheer quantity of this influence makes it important.

Second, school is the major arena in which children learn to deal with their peers. With very few exceptions, family relations always involve age differences. At school children deal with a large group of age mates, and this interaction is essential to their social formation.

Although emotions cannot be dictated by policy, there can be little doubt that the expectations and rules of the school environment create a set of obstacles and boundaries in which the emotional development of students takes place. In view of this it is important to ask what responsibility the school has for the emotional well-being of children.

It frequently happens that when students go through difficult times emotionally, both the home and the school begin to scrutinize each other as possible causes. I vividly recall being told by a teacher who had difficulty handling a contrary and sultry child, "I can spend my whole day trying to straighten him out, but it won't do a bit of good if he goes home every

1. The notion of task here must be understood broadly in the sense of nurture for right action. For a helpful discussion of this, see Nicholas Wolterstoff, *Educating for Responsible Action* (Grand Rapids: Eerdmans, 1980).

night and gets messed up again. Frankly, his happiness is beyond my control. I'd be happy if he'd just learn to read."[2]

Not all teachers dissociate themselves from the influences of a child's home. I have also been told by teachers that children are not in any shape to learn when things go badly at home; but these teachers do their best to compensate for children's home lives. They want school to be a refuge for unhappy children, a place where they can feel cared for and secure.

The examples just cited represent contrasting views of the school's responsibility for emotional development. The one assumes that the three R's take priority over everything else, and that even if a child's emotional well-being is in jeopardy, it is no reason for being distracted from the basics.

The other view assumes that children learn only when they are on balance emotionally. Thus, emotional well-being takes priority over basic skills for the simple reason that emotional well-being is a prerequisite to successful learning.

Some might even go so far as to say that being well-adjusted takes priority over being literate. After all, what would you rather be, literate and wretched or illiterate and happy? The problem with such a choice is, of course, that it makes mutually exclusive alternatives of what ought to be quite compatible outcomes of education.

Perhaps we need to face up to the fact that teachers cannot be everything. They cannot be parents or psychotherapists. But there are some things that schools are optimally designed to accomplish, and among these ought to be dealing with those matters that occur during the school day and in the school environment.

Schools are responsible for the teaching and learning of academic skills and the wholesome interaction of students with schoolmates and school staff. These are the tasks of the school environment.

It does not work for the school to try to compensate for what happens to a child at home. It is far more helpful if the

2. One of the best-known schemes for objectives in education is the taxonomy developed by B. S. Bloom. In the taxonomy Bloom distinguishes an affective domain from a cognitive domain. This is frequently translated by educators to mean an emotional emphasis on the one hand and an intellectual one on the other.

school staff does its very best to make the school, as school, a healthy place, so that regardless of what children face upon returning to their homes, their school day has been as whole-some as possible.

In short, a healthy educational atmosphere is one that en-courages children to be the best they can be in that environ-ment, without requiring that they be model children or come from model and uneventful households. This requires a system of limits set by a sense of regard for the well-being of others (students and staff) and respect for the importance of academic goals.

We will begin the following discussion by exploring the emotional component of the interaction students have with their fellow students. Then, we will consider the relationships of students with teachers. In that section we will reflect on the emotional exchanges children have with authority figures whose relationships with children are task oriented.

Finding a Place Among Equals

At school, as compared with home, the ratio of children to adults is much more heavily loaded in the direction of chil-dren. The influence of age mates is an especially significant factor in the school setting. Teachers are not directly involved in this peer network, but they do have some power over the circumstances under which it is formed and the limits within which it operates.

Social comparison. From the very first day children enter school they begin an intense program of social comparison. They pick out children like whom they wish to be; others they single out as children like whom they do not wish to be. Fellow students become a standard of comparison by which children judge whether they themselves are acceptable.

The process of social comparison often goes unnoticed un-less it poses problems. No teacher likes to hear a student ex-cuse an unkindness toward another student by explaining that no one likes the victim and everyone is unkind to him or her. At such times teachers are likely to warn students that what everyone else does should make no difference and they should think for themselves.

There is another more positive side to the process of social comparison. Especially on an emotional level, the assurance that others have felt the same feelings is often a very important ingredient. A child needs to muster enough courage to deal with those feelings, or to enable him to admit having the feelings so as to get help with them. Here is an example.

Almost every student has felt shy or timid at some time or other. However, students who are shy are likely to believe they are alone in this. Once a student feels odd because of having an emotion, the original problem has multiplied into two. The one is the feeling of timidity that was there in the first place, and the other is the worry about being strange or not as good as everyone else.

Counselors and therapists know all too well how adults still carry around feelings from childhood that have been shrouded in shame for years, because as children they were convinced they were the only ones who had such silly feelings. It is important that children be allowed to test and resolve their feelings by communicating with other children who are in the same circumstances and may have the same feelings.

Once students discover that others have had similar feelings, they have better access to models for handling their feelings—the models being those children who have also handled them. And the student who grapples with negative emotions thereby finds a valuable source of support. It is hard to take advice to be courageous from someone who appears never to have had a timid moment; it is far easier to take courage from the support of someone who has been in the same bind.

In addition, one of the first steps to managing emotions is admitting to having them. Students, who in the process of social comparison become convinced that they are the only ones who have felt the way they do, spend a good deal of their energy hiding their feelings from others and sometimes even from themselves.

Let us take as our example a student who goes to school the first day after transferring to a new school. It is intimidating to enter a new situation as a stranger when everyone else seems to be familiar and at ease.

The insightful teacher may help the new student considerably by acknowledging that it is difficult to begin attending a new school, by perhaps telling of his or her own experience with this, and by asking other students which of them have ever gone to a new school.

The opportunity for social comparison allows the new student to discover that others have also experienced being the new one. It allows the more seasoned students to remember when they were in the uncomfortable situation of being the new students and how much a friendly gesture or an offer of help could mean.

What difference does this exercise in social comparison make? It may save the new student from walking around the school pretending to be either disinterested or already familiar with it, both of which cover-up actions would put off any attempts by other students to be friendly. And social comparison may help experienced students to see through the newcomer's defenses and open the way for them to offer some welcoming help.

Examples of social comparison and peer support are multiplied many times over in the ordinary classroom. Each teacher must make some careful judgments in terms of the age and character of the classroom and how appropriate it is to draw attention to the emotional state of one particular student.

Teachers far too quickly assume that the younger the students the less well they can handle the distress of others. However, it is often the case that young students are more willing than older students to let the teacher guide the process of social comparison for them, because younger students are less inhibited about showing their more sensitive emotions. Furthermore, the more frequently a class acknowledges emotions the more comfortable students and teachers become with this.

It is certainly worth considering the value of emotional acknowledgment and peer support when students experience loss through death or divorce in the family, when younger children are upset by a parent's absence, or when the family profile changes because of the birth of a sibling or the death of a grandparent. Similarly, social comparison is helpful when a child has gone through distress because of illness or hospitalization, or when there are events in the community that cause children to feel worried or upset.

Empathy. As students learn to read the emotions of other students, they exercise the skills necessary for viewing a situation from another's point of view. And as they are able to separate their own situation from that of another they are also able to see more of the subtleties of social interaction.

It appears to observers of the social interactions of preschool children that most children assume that another child involved in the same situation as they will feel just the same way about it as they. It takes both intellectual and emotional maturity for children to realize that the way things appear from their own point of view may be quite different from the way they appear to someone else.

One way to encourage children to take social responsibility for their own actions is to teach them to identify the consequences of their emotional expressions on others. The development of such empathy is a critical ingredient in helping students to show consideration for each other in the classroom. Once again let us consider an example.

Suppose there is a classroom in which children have gotten into a pattern of teasing and upsetting each other with name calling and insults. The teacher of this classroom might simply make a rule that any child who insults another with name calling will have to stand in the corner, stay after school, or give up a favored activity.

By making social rules, teachers communicate clearly to children that there are categories of behavior that are acceptable and categories that are not. But will the teacher's rule convince the children that the behavior is also one that they themselves ought no longer approve?

Children who tease are usually experimenting with the social power that they exercise over each other. If they can upset or intimidate someone else, they feel powerful, even if the power is socially unacceptable. So, when children are infatuated with the social power that teasing achieves, they are probably quite indifferent to the actual pain their teasing causes its victims. They see the victim's pain, and realize they can cause it, but they do not actually empathize with the pain; that is, they cannot extend their imaginations far enough to know what it is like to be the teased one.

If teachers wish to alter the social interactions of children, it is more effective to build empathy than to interpose a teacher-centered rule. Suppose the teacher asked the teaser to come to the front of the room, and while the rest of the class looked on, directed the victim to now insult the teaser with the same unkind comments that had originally been the teaser's invention. And further suppose that the teacher encouraged the rest of the class to laugh at the teaser. What would happen?

We might venture to guess that some empathy would be established in one of two possible directions. In the one direction it is possible that the teaser would be humiliated by the insults and the class's laughter, and gain some sense of the victim's distress. In this case the teacher would instruct the victim that the next time he is bothered by the teaser's insults, it might help to remind the teaser how he looked standing up in front of the room taking his own medicine.

But it is also possible that the teaser would not be bothered at all by being made a spectacle. The teaser might simply toughen up and shrug off the insults. In this case the victim would find a new model with whom to empathize, and the teacher could remind the class that the insults ought simply to be ignored because even the teaser himself did not take them very seriously.

Whether the teaser were bothered or not by the turned tables that the teacher created in order to help the victim, child-centered outcomes are probably more effective than teacher-centered rules. Thus, teachers should be encouraged to be inventive in building empathy to regulate social interaction between students.

Interacting with Authority Figures

Effective task mediators are real people. Just as it is important for parents to develop the ability to express both their positive and negative feelings to their children, so it is important for teachers to be able to express both sides of their own emotion in their interactions with students.

However, teachers fall into habits of expressing some but not all of their emotional reactions, because they have an image to maintain with their students. Some teachers wish to have a nice-guy image. They are flattering, upbeat, and positive with their students. However, if a student makes such a teacher angry, or disappoints her teacher by being irresponsible, the nice-guy teacher is at a loss to respond.

Students are clever; they discover quickly where the weakness is in a teacher's emotional range. I was vividly impressed by this one time when I conducted a counseling group of junior-high-school students who had been identified by teachers and administrators as discipline problems. One teacher came up frequently as the topic of very angry conversation. They called him the beast.

The beast never smiled. He prided himself in taking no nonsense from students, and no matter what happened in his classroom he could carry on and complete his lesson as planned. All the students who had been identified as discipline problems were failing his class. They never missed the class, and almost never misbehaved there, because they did not dare. However, they boycotted the class intellectually by refusing to learn.

One of the things that became clear in conversations about the beast was that not only did the students get no passing grades from him, but also that they did not want to get passing grades from him. To get a passing grade from the beast would have been a mark of dishonor. The students were armored against the beast's criticism, and they had long ago lost any hope of winning his approval.

This example should not be taken as a suggestion that teachers smother their students with praise and flattery. Students also catch on very quickly to the imbalance of too much niceness. How can you trust the compliments of persons who lack the courage to criticize? Junior and senior high-school students can be viciously intolerant of teachers who are too nice.

What students need more than either positive and irrelevant feedback, or stern and arbitrary discipline, is honest reactions from adults who can be straightforward with a whole range of feelings and emotions. Students need this emotional richness, because they count on others to be mirrors in which they can see and evaluate themselves along the whole range of negative to positive emotions. In order to be able to trust the feelings about themselves that they gain from encounters with teachers, students need to sense the emotional richness and balance of their teachers.

Teachers manage a setting in which children play out a sig-

nificant part of their experience in dealing with persons outside the family. Teachers who do this well are persons who can
get beyond being empty or formal functionaries, and who dare
to be genuine and human with children.

Being genuine involves far more than what happens on an
emotional level. The teacher who is genuine with children is
the teacher who is willing to let students know who he or she
is, so that the teacher can model for the children what it means
to be an ethical person, one who is able to set goals and achieve
them, and one who can do all of these things in a wholesome
and constructive way.

PART 2

What Are the Background Theories?

8

The Academic Study
of Emotion

Academic discussion of emotion might remind us vaguely of a garden shrub. In growth seasons it rapidly fills out; in off seasons it gets trimmed back dramatically. The cycle goes on and on. Much of the discussion centers on defining what emotion is.

For example, at one time it was fashionable for psychologists to preoccupy themselves with cataloging types of emotion. They asked, "How many emotions are there?" They wanted to know whether the myriad words used to describe emotions refer to distinct emotional states, or whether there are just a few basic emotions, each of which has many fine nuances.

As fashions in psychological research changed, a new generation of psychologists thought it archaic to quibble about the number and names of emotions. New rules of research allowed only events that can be directly observed by scientists to be suitable for scientific investigation. This excluded private states or feelings. As a consequence, the study of emotion shifted toward a physiological emphasis because physiological states can be observed by scientists directly and do not depend on subjective reports of people scientists study. Enormous effort went into sorting and defining language, mental states, human capacities, and measurable physical events in the hope that out of it all would come a scientifically defensible view of emotion.

Overall, the psychological investigation of emotion has been laden with ambiguity, and much of the discussion has degenerated into purely academic debates. Ordinary people, convinced that they do have emotions, could find very little to persuade them that academic discussions of emotion had any relation to real, living, breathing people.

Once again, a wave of reaction set in, this time against the scientific method of dissembling recognizable emotions. The critics of that previous trend chose one of two directions. In one, the "pop psychology" movement thumbed its nose at scientific restrictions. It argued that if ordinary people can recognize their own experiences in what psychologists write about or speak about, that is a sufficient basis for assuming that these psychologists make sense and refer to something real.

Going in a somewhat different direction, other psychologists began to insist that some way must be found to give a precise scientific account of emotion, including its inner, or subjective, states. This presented a serious challenge to the whole discipline of psychology because there was a widely held agreement that the proper objects for psychologists to study are those which are "public." A public event is one that can be observed directly by *anyone* trained to observe it. But, of course, a person's private emotions or mental state are not observable this way and cannot be studied until the person reports them to the observer. These subjective reports were thought to be less satisfactory material for scientific study than other measures of emotion such as blood-pressure or damp palms. These signs of emotion can be studied directly by any scientist who has good equipment for doing so. In other words, these signs are public. Thus, the study of private mental states required relaxing some rules of method prized highly by many psychologists.

Thus, over time in the psychological study of emotion a diversity of approaches made its appearance. For each psy-

chologist making a claim there was another making an op-
posite or at least a contradictory claim.[1]

Where does the diversity and ambiguity in the scholarly
study of emotion leave those of us who want to reflect on the
matter of emotion, who do so primarily because we want to
discover how to live wholesomely with our own emotions and
because we want to do justice to the feelings of those with
whom we are in contact and upon whom we have influence—
family members, students, colleagues, friends, and those persons with whom we live in neighborhood, church, and community? Must we continue to hack our way through the thickets
of scientific discourse, hoping that we can come to some insight that will serve our simple day-to-day interests?

It is beyond the intention of this present discussion to sort
out the entire complex of issues that get tangled in philosophical and social-scientific studies of emotion. But it would also
be unwise for us to turn our backs on this work completely.[2]

Scientific views, although we may not be acquainted with
them on the theoretical level, have shaped the common-sense
views of emotion that we encounter in the mass media, in
teacher education, in well-meant advice to assist parents in
child rearing, and in books on self-help psychology. As con-
sumers we are inclined to adopt advice that is the offspring
of the grand theories of philosophers and social scientists, and
sometimes we do so without knowing anything at all about
the origin of such advice.

For the purposes of our reflections, it would seem both wise
and sufficient for us to focus on a few main elements from the
more complex scientific discussions of emotion. The most deliberate way of going about this is for us to begin by asking
three preliminary questions.

First, what are the most common views of emotion? Although there are literally hundreds of pieces of research on
emotion, they tend to fall in line with major schools of thought.
The various theories *within* a particular group may be distin-

1. A helpful review of the debates appears in Amelie Oksenberg Rorty,
ed., *Explaining Emotions* (Los Angeles: University of California, 1980).
2. For a philosophical discussion of emotion, see Robert C. Roberts, *Spir-
ituality and Human Emotion* (Grand Rapids: Eerdmans, 1982).

guished from one another in terms of how they develop sub-ordinate ideas, but they share certain major assumptions.

The following might be a crude parallel. Seasoned baseball fans may be convinced that Tiger Stadium and Yankee Stadium are not at all alike, but compare them to a football field and their similarities become quite apparent. In a similar fashion the various traditions or schools of research in psychology investigate the same subjects but do so in different ways. At first glance they may seem quite similar but the more carefully we examine the work of these distinct schools, the more significant their differences appear. We will explore these traditions in chapter 10.

Second, what do psychologists imply in their choice to accept and work with a certain view of emotion? There is always more involved in a psychological theory than is apparent from a condensed description of it. The methods a researcher uses for assembling observations and the categories used for constructing a theory are not chosen willy-nilly.

The ideas psychology theorists use come out of the traditions that have formed their scientific mindsets. Following in such traditions, these scientists accept a set of answers to pre-scientific questions such as: What is a person? What can we know about other persons? What are acceptable procedures for the way scientists argue a case?

We may get discouraged when we glimpse the complicated issues underlying what seems to be a simple theory. Brilliant scholars spend whole lifetimes discussing preliminary issues like the above. Someone might quite rightly object that if the scholars do a thorough job of exploring the assumptions underlying an approach to emotion, it may take so long they will never get around to considering the matter of emotion itself.

On the other hand, our ignoring the scientists' assumptions does not make them unimportant; it only makes us naive. I may refuse to look at the sky and admit that it is raining, but doing so will not keep the ground dry. Furthermore, it seems a good idea for us to clarify what assumptions matter most to *us*. Then we can examine the basic approaches of the psychologists' stance on their theories.

Third, against what measure do we evaluate the adequacy

of our inquiry? If it is unavoidable that our explorations are selective, it need not imply that they are either capricious or arbitrary. Our process of selection must be guided by a larger and more inclusive view into which we will incorporate our observations.

When we as Christians probe scientific schools of thought regarding emotion and their views of personhood, we will soon find ourselves out of the range of scientific inquiry and into considerations of another kind. For when we seek to understand the meaning of personhood we are dealing with deeply religious issues. To gain insight into these matters Christians turn to sacred Scripture. Essential to a Christian view of persons is what the gospel tells us about who we are, about God's intentions for us and about God's dealings with us in sacred history.

In the discussion in the following chapters we will move through a consideration of our preliminary questions, one at a time. In chapter 9 we will look at major scientific approaches to the study of emotion. In chapter 10 we will explore a religiously founded view of the person and consider how this view may serve as a guide for sifting through the findings of science in order to develop our own insights about healthy emotions.

The general views we will survey in this discussion are not intended to be foundations for an argument. If that were the case we would have to present them first and argue *from* them to specifics.

In this introductory discussion we have established the need for a mindset or a set of attitudes to guide the direction of our inquiry. In all discussions, guiding attitudes are operating, sometimes without being stated, and sometimes without even being *consciously* held by the participants in the discussion. The purpose, then, of what follows is to clarify those views that operate in the psychologists' discussion of emotion, and then to offer a Christian perspective in making our own comments on those views.

9

The Offerings of Science

The full body of psychological literature dealing with emotion is very extensive. In addition, disciplines other than psychology have explored the matter; for example, there are also extensive biological and philosophical bodies of literature on emotion. What we will survey here is necessarily sketchy; however, the goal of this survey is to present the primary thrust of four of the basic approaches to the psychological study of emotion.

The Ethological View

The ethological tradition in psychology is close kin to biology, especially to the line of inquiry that studies the complex behavioral patterns typical of a given species. For example, an ethologist, after observing many cases in which sending roses is part of human courting, might investigate whether monkeys also exchange objects as part of their courting habits.

Following the direction set forth by Charles Darwin's theory of evolution, psychological inquiry of this sort has worked on the assumption that the most important feature of all behavior is that it is either a help or a hindrance in the struggle for survival. The outcome of the struggle for survival is important to whether a particular individual survives or succumbs. But it is even more important because the survivors have those adaptive features that tend to become more and more characteristic of a species over the course of succeeding generations.

In 1975 Edward Wilson wrote *Sociobiology: The New Synthesis.*[1] In this book the author intended to bring Darwinism up to date. Evolutionists have always been hard pressed to explain how the apparently altruistic behavior of some humans, such as soldiers who sacrifice their lives in the defense of their country, could be consistent with the principle of survival of the fittest. After all, the young able-bodied soldiers who risk their lives and die are more fit than many of those in whose defense they act.

While maintaining the view that human beings are complex biological machines striving to survive, Wilson tried to explain some of these complex and puzzling social phenomena. It is not ourselves as individuals, but rather our genetic heritage that we are all trying to preserve, Wilson concluded, and thus our social behaviors are genetically (not individually) selfish.

Family commitments, racism, and wars are all examples of the natural drive to preserve persons most similar to us for the sake of giving them the advantage over persons less similar to us, in the persistent struggle for survival in which we are all engaged. Wilson's view seems to echo Darwin's sentiments about nature being "red in tooth and claw."

The ethological approach has also been a very important tradition in specialized psychological studies of emotion, and in this area it has taken two major tacks. One of them hails back to Darwin himself, who in 1892 published a book entitled: *The Expression of Emotions in Man and Animals.*[2] In this book Darwin claimed that emotions had an important role to play in the course of evolution. A well-known modern proponent of Darwin's view is Paul Eckman, a researcher who has conducted extensive cross-cultural studies on emotional expression. He assumes that facial expressions, bodily pos-

1. Edward O. Wilson, *Sociobiology: The New Synthesis* (Cambridge: Harvard University, 1975).
2. Charles Darwin, *The Expression of Emotions in Man and Animals* (New York: D. Appleton, 1897).

tures, and bodily movements are all essential to the human species as simple forms of social communication.

One function of emotional expression, says Eckman, is to indicate internal states, with the result that the behavior of the one giving the expression is more predictable. For example, we would be more likely to expect attack from someone wearing an angry frown than from someone wearing a relaxed smile.

A second function of emotional expression, according to the ethological point of view, is to reflect to others the state of the environment. We feel at ease when entering a room whose occupants have their heads thrown back in laughter. We have quite another feeling upon entering a room whose occupants are leaning forward, have their shoulders rounded, and are wringing their hands.

When we see someone else's expression, we assume that this person is reacting to "something," and his emotional expression gives us some hints about how we must prepare to react to that "something." It is interesting that emotional communication lets us prepare to react before we even know to what particular object or event we are reacting.

Based on his extensive studies, Eckman has suggested that there are certain basic emotional expressions found in every human group. Nevertheless, these universal patterns may also show some variations from group to group. For example, when Eckman studied emotional expression in American and Japanese university students, he found a greater tendency among Japanese than among Americans to mask distress with polite smiles.

In summary, Eckman's research indicates that while certain basics of emotion seem to be transmitted genetically, the particulars of their expression may also be shaped by social influence.[3]

A second tack which the ethological approach in psychology has taken pertains to the relationship between the brain (how it is built and how it works) and patterns of emotional behavior. All researchers who do comparative studies of animal brains agree that mammals have more complex brains than other animals.

On the basis of these comparative studies, many researchers

3. Paul Eckman and W. Firesen, *Unmasking the Face* (Englewood Cliffs: Prentice-Hall, 1975).

conjecture that the brains of higher animals became more complex over a long period of time. They suggest that gradually, in the course of evolution, new parts of the brain developed in addition to older and more primitive parts. Based on this view, certain areas deep inside the human brain are referred to as the primitive brain.

Paul McLean is a psychologist who has studied the design of the human brain relative to emotional behavior. Based upon his findings, McLean offers the notion of a "triune brain." He suggests that the experience and expression of emotion in humans involves three distinct but complexly related areas of the brain. Each area has a structure and a chemistry unlike that of the others, and McLean believes that they also developed at different times in the course of evolution.

According to McLean, rabbits, cats, monkeys and humans all have distinctive patterns of emotion because they represent different levels on the hierarchy of development that emerged over millions of years. Of all these, the human brain is the most highly differentiated; furthermore, this is reflected in the fact that humans also have the most highly differentiated emotions.[4]

Ethological approaches to psychology come in many more forms than the few cited here, but these should suffice to give the reader an initial impression of the emphasis of this group of theories. What all of them have in common is the assumption that the most significant insights regarding behavior are to be had by considering the struggle to survive of both individuals and the entire species. What we are is what our ancestors became as they adapted in order to prevail in the timeless struggle of the species against nature.

The practical applications to emotion that issue from an ethological view carry out the theme of the utility of behavior in the service of survival. Thus, when judging the desirability of a certain emotional pattern, ethologists do not ask whether it is good or bad, right or wrong, civil or uncouth, pleasant or miserable. Instead, they ask upon what ancestral patterns the

4. Paul McLean, "Contrasting Function of Limbic and Neocortical Systems of the Brain and Their Relevance to Psychophysiological Aspects of Medicine," *American Journal of Medicine* 25 (1958): 611–26.

behavior is based and what purpose this pattern serves in the species's survival.

Consider the case of the playground bully who goes around most of the time with a curled lip, and who leaves intimidated victims in his wake. The ethologist's first questions would not have to do with this child's unhappiness or the distress of the other children; nor would the ethologist ask whether this situation is ethically acceptable. Instead, the ethologist would begin with a consideration of human aggression and its role in preserving the species, and would then evaluate the children's ecosystem in terms of this more general pattern.

Is it the case that the member of the group who establishes power and aggression within the group may also be the most aggressive in defending the group from outside attack? This is the pattern, after all, in monkey colonies. What are the instinctive mechanisms that regulate the bully's threats and the other children's fear? What is the total social network of playground relations?

The psychologist who believes that social interaction and emotional expression come about in the course of the struggle for survival usually is slow to suggest that we should tamper with "naturally" occurring social systems. Tampering with social systems by thoughtlessly changing the behavior of one member is analogous to disrupting the ecosystem by "cutting down a few forests." There is a hidden sequence of events set loose in a domino effect when we begin to meddle.

Some, but only a few, ethological psychologists would insist that it is best to let the chips fall where they may. While in theory allowing the weak to eliminate themselves may be the shortest course to the best level of adaptation for the greatest number, this view violates the human and liberal values of most social scientists. These same social scientists are quick to suggest, however, that some of the most troublesome patterns of human emotion are a product of our inept tampering in the first place.

The Psychoanalytic View

The approach to psychology that originated with Sigmund Freud represents a revolutionary turn in modern thought. Un-

til the time of Freud, the understanding of human motivation
and emotion had been dominated by a rationalist tradition.
The assumption had been that we act toward the world in
terms of how we understand it, and that we choose one action
over against another by determining which is most reasonable.

Freud shattered the conventional belief in rationality and
in its place put the view that humans are driven by irrational
forces. Although he did allow for the possibility that the powers of rationality can make some gain on irrationality, he also
maintained that the gain of rationality represents but a small
margin of the total forces directing human behavior, and furthermore that the gain is made only with the greatest effort.
The method he recommended for bringing irrationality to trial
in the court of reason was his own psychoanalytic method.[5]

In psychoanalytic theory, instincts and feelings are closely
related, but we must not make the mistake of assuming that
they are identical. Instincts are those forces in individuals that
push them to pursue pleasure and avoid pain. Thus we seek
food when hungry, rest when tired, relief when under stress,
protection when threatened, etc. If we succeed in satisfying
our instinctual needs, positive feelings result.

Human infants, according to Freud, give themselves entirely
to the instinctual pursuit of pleasure. In his lectures on psychoanalysis Freud saw great significance in the fact that infants will wail for nourishment with no regard to whom they
may disturb or what they may disrupt. Parents of newborns
know how little ones will do this with unrestrained vehemence
in the wee hours of the morning. Similarly, infants will fill
their diapers with no concern for the dignity of their company;
mother or queen, father or king—it is all the same to a baby.

Babies also make demands for the comfort of company
without reserve. Once infants have learned that if they cry
someone will pick them up, there is no explaining to them that
they should be less demanding because there are other children in the family or important tasks to which attention needs
to be given. Babies, in Freud's view, are instinctual tyrants.

Instinct is not allowed to go unchecked very long, however,

5. Sigmund Freud, *A General Introduction to Psychoanalysis* (New York:
Liveright, 1935).

not even in babies. Observations about the bald instinctiveness of babies was not the end of Freud's theory, either. While infants are still newcomers to this world, parents begin to schedule their eating, sleeping, and socializing in such a fashion as to make the fulfilling of the infants' needs more compatible with everyone else's. And within a few years infants become toilet trained, aware of yes and no, and remarkably civilized.

The result of the process of civilization, according to psychoanalytic theory, is a collision of forces that battle for priority within the children themselves. On the one hand, the instincts, directed by the pleasure principle, make claims on children's attention and action. Freud called these forces the "id." But on the other hand, all this while, the will of the parents, and through them the will of society, is reining in the instincts. This Freud called the "superego."

Eventually children, by identifying with parents, make the parents' standards their own. With this development the individual psyche is truly a house divided against itself. The instinctual energy the obedient child or civilized adult stifles gives rise in turn to negative feelings: anger, jealousy, fear, anxiety, and shame.

The instinctive energy that gets restrained by the superego may come to various ends. One possibility is for it to find indirect expression through civilized means that accomplish the same instinctive ends. Dreams may allow the fulfillment of childish wishes in ways that the real world would never allow. Or, a tyrannical parent may shunt onto children the vengeance that was meant for, but never expressed toward, his or her own punishing parent. And this displaced anger may even be rationalized by the earnest conviction that discipline (even when harsh and arbitrary) is good for children, because they are allowed to be too soft these days.

A second possible way of handling instinctive energy that gets held back is to pretend that it does not exist. In this case it stays within the person and breeds uneasiness and discomfort. Being on guard to keep criminal wishes imprisoned requires a considerable expenditure of energy. That is why depressive people are exhausted. Furthermore, these imprisoned feelings may sneak out when the guard is down. When your tongue gets twisted and you call your mother-in-law "mugger," it might just be that you mean it.[6]

The psychoanalytic view of the person, and the view of emotion that goes with it, is also tied in with a particular view of what we must do to live well with our feelings. The positive ones are no problem, of course. But the negative ones that have come about through the blockage of our instincts are the psychoanalyst's real concern.

The treatment of these negative feelings is not easy, because in the process of the collision between id and superego the true instinctive impulses have been elaborately covered over by deceits and denials. In fact, so thick is the deception that even the deceiver probably no longer knows the way out of the maze.

One of the basic tenets of psychoanalytic treatment is that we can never take people's actions at face value. The hidden meaning of our actions is always more important than the apparent meaning. Thus, if the psychoanalyst were asked to deal with the playground bully, the first questions would be concerned with the hidden motives of this child's behavior.

Perhaps it is some frustration at home that causes a child to be aggressive at school. Maybe this child's basic needs for approval and security are not being met. Perhaps bullying is a form of attention seeking or a cover of deep insecurity. In any case, before any corrective can be attempted, the deep and hidden complications of the bully's psyche must be unearthed by the skilled archeology of the keen analyst.

The Humanistic View

Humanistic psychology is often referred to as the third force in psychology. It is a reaction against psychoanalysis and against the hard-nosed scientific approaches in psychology that overlooked the ways in which humans are distinct from animals. It claims to have a far more optimistic view of the self than these other approaches have.

Third force theories have sometimes been called self-theo-

---

6. Sigmund Freud, *The Psychopathology of Everyday Life* (New York: Norton, 1965).

ries. Their major emphasis is that the worth and dignity of every individual must come to free and spontaneous expression. Understanding how this may be accomplished is a concern that, according to this view, should be first and foremost in the psychologist's efforts.

Carl Rogers, one of the leading proponents of humanistic psychology, has proposed that every person lives in a world of experience of which the self is the center. The image that each person has of him or herself is an assemblage built out of profound emotional experiences.

Each of us needs love and approval. If we are accepted as we are without conditions, then we become expressive, flexible, and creative. However, if those from whom we seek love make conditional demands on us ("I will love you if you do as I wish"), we run a great risk of becoming artificial. For the sake of love we may pretend to be what we are not and to act in ways that contradict our deepest feelings, but it is a no-win game. In the end we become empty and confused, our actions entirely determined by outside influences.[7]

A major source of psychological handicaps is the damage done as a result of living by someone else's agenda. Healthy people live by their own wishes. Because the humanistic psychologist believes that human nature is basically good, it follows that living by their own wishes will lead people to constructive ends. Destructiveness toward self and others comes about when persons continually get tangled up in contradictions between their own wishes and the expectations of others. When the mismatch becomes extreme, emotional reactions become unpredictable and anxiety increases exponentially.

Because humanistic psychologists believe that unhappy people already suffer from being overpowered by others, the approach they recommend for dealing with emotions is to create a climate for free expression. In a warm and accepting relationship with someone who offers support but makes no demands, the distressed individual can finally try out those feelings that have not been previously allowed.[8]

We can speculate how humanistic psychologists would deal

7. Carl Rogers, *On Becoming Persons* (Boston: Houghton Mifflin, 1961).
8. Carl Rogers, *Client-Centered Therapy* (Boston: Houghton Mifflin, 1951).

with a child's aggressive feelings without disapproving of those feelings. Instead of telling her that picking on other children makes them dislike her, the helpful humanistic psychologist would begin by mirroring the bully's aggression back to her: "You look angry enough to pound somebody." In the volley of expression and response the therapist would help the child discover more constructive ways of dealing with her distressing emotion.

Understanding one's own emotion is a key ingredient of humanistic psychology, because body states, emotional expression, habitual gestures, and even illness may be statements about a person's inner state. Those who have learned to deny their own feelings have come to feel empty, helpless, bewildered, and lonely. Therefore, before they can get back on the track to self-fulfillment, they must learn to understand the language of their own feelings.[9]

The Cognitive View

One of the oldest views of emotion coalesces with one of the most popular views. It is the notion that feelings are products of our interpretations of the world. For example, if I encounter a great, lumbering sheep dog and judge it to be powerful and unpredictable, I may feel afraid. But if I see that same animal as our friendly, family pet, then the greatest threat from it may be a slobbering nuzzle in the face. In the latter case I am more likely to feel friendly than afraid. What is the difference between these two cases? The differences in my feelings would depend on the way I construe the event.

In western culture there has been a long tradition of suspicion regarding emotion. Reason, according to the views of many respected thinkers, can be trusted, but emotion may divert and deceive us. Thus, reason must be used to control emotion, and the ability to place reason above emotion is the

9. Within the humanistic psychology movement there has been some important recognition that this process is not merely an intellectual one. For example, Alexander Lowen has insisted that rehabilitation must begin by an exploration and then retraining of the language of the body. See A. Lowen, *Physical Dynamics of Character: Bodily Form and Movement in Analytic Therapy* (New York: Grune and Statton, 1958).

mark of the virtuous person. The squaring off of emotion over against reason is a theme that may be found in writings by such renowned thinkers as Aristotle, Thomas Aquinas, and Immanuel Kant.

But when we speak of the cognitivists' approach to emotion as one of the major approaches, we are not referring specifically to the old rationalists' view. In order to understand how a new form of cognitivism emerged on the psychological scene, we need to trace the sequence of some important events in the history of the study of emotion.

While a very optimistic and respectful view of rationality held sway during the seventeenth and eighteenth centuries, by the nineteenth century there were some strong reactions in the other direction. Objections against ultimate confidence in reason were posed, for the most part, by thinkers who believed that the highest human capacity is not reason but will. Those powers within that push us along toward goals and the energy and vitality to pursue our wishes—these are the unique features of human nature. We have already encountered variations on this theme in Freud (the will to pleasure) and in Darwin (the will to survive).

Now in the twentieth century there is a swing away from these anti-rationalist views of psychology and toward understanding human beings and their actions in terms of the way they think and the way they construe their worlds. In psychology this trend is called cognitivism; in the study of emotion it is often referred to as constructivism. These approaches assume that the way we act and react is dependent on the way we think. Our behavior cannot be understood apart from the categories within which we construct our experiences.

What does all of this have to do with emotion? Well, emotion also comes about as a product of our interpretations. One of the most ingenious demonstrations of this process of interpretation was conducted by the social psychologist Stanley Schachter.[10] Many theories of emotion take into account the idea that emotional experience is made up of both a state of physical arousal and a state of mental awareness. Schachter

10. Stanley Schachter and J. Singer, "Cognitive, Social, and Physiological Determinants of Emotional State," *Psychological Review* 69 (1979): 379–99.

speculated that the physical state is an undifferentiated one—a sort of raw material for the emotional experience—but that the physical state comes to be experienced as a particular emotion only after the individual has interpreted the environmental situation and attributed the state of his physical arousal to something.

In order to test his theory with a laboratory demonstration, Schachter asked volunteers to take part in an experiment, the ostensive purpose of which was a study of vision. Information about the real purpose of the experiment was withheld from the participants. Under the pretext that they were being given an injection of vitamins, the participants were actually injected with a synthetic form of adrenalin that works on the autonomic nervous system and produces a state of excitation.

Some of the participants in Schachter's experiment were correctly told that the injection they had been given might have side effects such as increased heart rate, clammy palms, nervousness. Other participants were either told nothing or were misinformed as to the side effects.

After being injected, the participants were asked to wait in a room until they could be given a vision test. In this same room was one of the experimenter's assistants, who pretended to be another participant. With some participants the assistant behaved in a silly fashion, while in the presence of others he acted angry.

Those participants who had prior information about the side effects of the injection believed the behavior of the experimenter's assistant had very little effect on their emotional states; however, those participants who had not been correctly informed as to the effects of the drug tended to attribute their agitated state to the behavior of the assistant—feeling angry when the assistant acted angry and feeling silly when that was how the assistant behaved.

From this research and other studies along the same lines, Schachter concluded that a state of physical excitement is a necessary condition for the general experience of emotion, but the particular emotion experienced is a result of the individual's cognitive evaluation of the situation. In short, he held that our emotions are influenced by the categories of the terms in which we interpret our world.

The four major views of emotion we have reviewed are each rooted in a major perspective operating in the field of psychology today. These differing perspectives are in turn part and parcel of grand theories with strongly committed answers to the question "What is a person?"

The ethological view emphasizes adaptation and survival. Not only are the behaviors of individuals explained in this fashion, but the habitual patterns of the species are as well. Thus, the conclusion of this view is that organic, emotional, and social structures and functions are all part of the same adaptive scheme and have come to their present form over the long course of evolution.

The psychoanalytic view emphasizes the instinctive pursuit of pleasure (the id) as it comes into conflict with the restraining forces of society (the superego). Satisfied needs yield pleasure and positive emotion; frustrated needs yield distress and negative emotion.

The humanistic view emphasizes the free, creative goodness of every individual. When the inner self comes to spontaneous expression, satisfaction and positive emotion result. When the self is discredited and expression denied, neurosis and distress result.

The cognitive view emphasizes the mental construction of the world, a process that is constantly being carried on as persons act on and in the world. Emotion is one product of these attempts to interpret the world.

When we survey the bodies of literature that deal with emotion, we accumulate an array of ideas, all of which do not fit together easily into an integrated whole. Some of the assumptions made by theorists of each persuasion cast doubt on the claims made by theorists of the other persuasions.

Were it the case that each theoretical approach only drew together an assemblage of evidence, then we might expect that it should be possible to construct one overview that would draw all the various sorts of evidence together. However, the task is not quite so straightforward.

Each of the major views of emotion includes some evidence, but also, more importantly, an interpretation of that evidence. These interpretations are attempts on the part of the theorists to go beyond their evidence and to explain its significance.

Ideas about emotion in each of these theoretical approaches are woven into an image of the person. And this image is intended to be not only a reflection of our emotions, but, more profoundly, of ourselves as persons.

Can science tell us what a person is? Probably not. Science can give us some information about how persons behave, or think, or feel. But what a person *is* remains a mystery.

However, the Christian asking what a person is has another source, a more original one, for getting a glimpse of insight into this profound question. Scripture tells us about ourselves as persons.

When Christians draw together their scientific reflections, they also do so in the context of a religious view of persons. While they may elaborate this view in the course of their scientific inquiry, it is founded in what their faith asserts it to be. The founding of our views and the elaboration of them are two different matters. When we Christians develop our views, it is essential that we distinguish between the two.

10

A Sacred View of Persons

The view of the person with which a Christian comes to a discipline such as psychology is rooted in religious belief; it is a view he or she has learned from the Bible and the traditional teachings of the church. Nonetheless, a Christian view of the person is not an antiscientific view. On the contrary, it is protoscientific, for it is a view that existed before science, and it provides a context that makes the scientific enterprise a meaningful one.

A religious view of the person is not constructed in a theory; it is revealed in a story. The story narrates an overarching view of past and future, and central to its plot is the relationship of humans with the divine. Most significantly, it is everyone's story.

When we look to Scripture to find an answer to the question of the meaning of persons, we find a story about a person who is a creature. A creature is a "created one," and this human creature is made in God's image.

Often in the history of Christian philosophy and theology, this notion of image has been taken to mean that human beings share in certain of God's traits while animals do not. In particular, the capacities to will and reason have been singled out as those which are especially godlike.[1] But Scripture gives a still more profound meaning to the idea of image.

The Scriptures tell us to love God with heart, soul, mind, and strength—that is, entirely. In the world that God created, that was not marred by sin, humankind imaged God by willing rightly and by knowing truly, not merely by willing and reasoning per se. What is most essential to the image of God in us, and thus to our definition as persons, is the relationship of God the creator with us the creatures he made.

The perfect harmony in which we—humans—were created, the story goes on to tell us, was not only a perfect harmony with the creator, but also perfect harmony among all the creatures God made. The image of paradise is one in which each creature had a place among all the others. And the place of the original man and woman was to be special caretakers of the other creatures that the Lord had made.

The second chapter of Genesis recounts that "The Lord God took the man and put him in the Garden of Eden to work it and take care of it" (Gen. 2:15). The narrative further tells us that after forming the beasts of the field and the birds of the air, the Lord brought them to the man to see what he would name them, and the names the man gave to them were the names by which the beasts and birds continued to be called.

Finally, the story in Genesis tells us that the original person was not meant to be alone, but that man and woman were made for a special partnership, so closely united that they were called one flesh. And it was to this whole creation of heavens and earth, all living things, and the original human partnership that the Lord God gave a blessing.

There is more to the story of our relationship with the creator and with the creatures as it is told in Scripture. Not only does it tell of our origin and the purpose of our existence, but it also tells how our knowledge of ourselves has been clouded and how our relationship with the creator has been damaged.

From the Genesis narrative of humanity's fall into sin, we learn that our relationship with God was broken because we were not content to be creatures, but wanted to be godlike.

1. For a presentation of this view, see R. Koteskey, *Psychology from a Christian Perspective* (Nashville: Abingdon, 1980).

The price of usurping God's glory was that we became thoroughly corrupted—knowing evil as well as good. Everything in us and about us was touched by the distorting consequences of sin: our wills became corrupt, our understanding blurred, our human relationships stressful, our guardianship of the other creatures unreliable, our feelings bent, and our actions inadequate.

Just as the perfect harmony of the original creation was both a harmony of the creatures with the creator and of the creatures with each other, so the scars that marred the relationship of humankind with God also marred the relationship of all things created with each other.

So the principal actors were set in opposition to each other. The tragic recitation of the third chapter of Genesis tells how humankind was alienated from the earth ("Cursed is the ground because of you"), how humankind was alienated from the animals and destined to struggle in a relationship marked by enmity, how man and woman would be caught in the conflict of power and desire, and even how the relation of woman to her offspring would be marked by pain.

The earth was so corrupted that eventually God grieved that he had made it, and determined to send a flood to destroy it.

> Now the earth was corrupt in God's sight and full of violence.
> . . . So God said to Noah: "I am going to put an end to all people,
> for the earth is filled with violence because of them. I am surely
> going to destroy both them and the earth (Gen. 6:11–12).

Fortunately, God's wrath and the flood are not the end of God's dealings with us.

The story of the flood is followed by a renewal of God's promises and an offer of grace that brings hope to all God's creatures who are alienated from each other. In the story of Noah we are told how far reaching God's promises of renewal are. When Noah brought his sacrifices to the altar, God promised him that the ground would never be cursed again because of what people do. And never again, God promised, would all the living creatures be destroyed.

God made those promises to Noah in spite of human evil. As long as the earth endures, seedtime and harvest, cold and heat, summer and winter, day and night will never cease. The rainbow is stretched across the sky as a sign of this promise, and God gives this assurance: "This is the sign of the covenant I am making between me and you and every living creature with you, a covenant for all generations to come" (Gen. 9:12).

The Scriptures also tell us of Christ's work for and in us by which our relationship with the creator is still being renewed in a process that is not yet complete. Thus we see that what we are as persons is not only defined by our relationship with God, but also that this relationship has gone through a dramatic process, beginning with its creation as a perfect harmony, then its being bent by sin, and now its restoration. Our relationship with God is marked out in salvation history. Sacred history also marks out our relationships with others and our place in the creation.

What does all of this have to do with such human activities as feeling, thinking, struggling to survive, preferring pleasure to pain, and all the others we might name? It gives them a context and puts them into proper perspective. All of these sides of human events refer to ways we act, things we do, and capacities we have, but the story of salvation history tells us who most essentially we are.

The person as self only has ultimate meaning in relation to the creator. It is this relationship that makes us whole. In the breaking of it we become incomplete, and in the renewal of it we have the promise of being made whole again. The definition of persons is relational, and it is ultimately religious.

This accounting of ourselves sounds very different from the kinds of statements about ourselves that come by way of science. But what is the relationship between these two kinds of knowledge?

There has been a strong tendency among Christians studying the sciences to assume that science can be accepted as it is, and that Christian faith is then added to the deliverances of science in order to sanctify them.[2] If we take seriously our meaning of persons as those who are defined by a relationship with God and whose identities have been transformed in sal-

2. For an example of this, see Rodger Bufford, *The Human Reflex: Behavioral Psychology in Biblical Perspective* (San Francisco: Harper and Row, 1981).

vation history, then this explanation of the relation of science to faith is not adequate.

What we must first see is that it is not scientific views that are basic, but rather that faith is basic and that scientific work takes place in the context of it. Faith reflects the overarching meaning of existence; science can give only a partial account of specific events.

The major psychological perspectives we reviewed in the last chapter are not set in the context of self-knowledge by faith. In fact, in some cases they deny the deepest religious meaning of existence. Each of these views ignores or denies the relationship of the creature with the creator, and each proceeds on the assumption that persons can be understood adequately in terms of themselves and their world, just as they are.

Sacred history, however, cannot be added to or omitted from perspectives based on personal taste. When a religious definition of the person is omitted, another principle to account for the identity of persons and the course of human history must be found. This is where the secular mindset and the mindset radically founded in faith differ most essentially.

For, according to the secular mindset, religion is a mythic system that is superimposed on a neutral reality for the purposes of explanation. However, the mindset radically founded in faith assumes that the sacred is real and everywhere present. Thus, an explanation of human events that intentionally fails to consider the sacred, commits itself to a studied ignorance of something basic to reality.

But it does more than this; it also focusses on another principle of ultimacy by which to account for the whole meaning of persons and the course of human history. Earlier we observed four psychological perspectives that have taken a dimension of behavior as a point of orientation. For the ethologist it is the struggle to survive, for the psychoanalyst the pursuit of instinctive pleasure, for the humanistic psychologist the freedom and fulfillment of self-expression, and for the cognitivist the powers of the mind to construct an understanding of the world. In each one, some facet of human experience is made absolute.

When seen against the counterpoint of the Christian under-

standing, we find that in each of the major scientific perspectives some functional side of human activity has been made
into a principle in terms of which human nature is defined.
This principle thus replaces for those scientists the relationship of humans to the divine that in sacred history defines
what human beings are. Secular views of the person are de-
rivative views—derived from but also reactions against the
more profound knowledge of self that comes through a faith
nurtured in sacred traditions.

We should not make the mistake now of overreacting to the
denials implicit in secular psychology so that we turn our
backs on those events for which they are attempted accounts.
The denial of God does not destroy God, nor does the failure
to acknowledge the creation as the Lord's obliterate it. After
all, God once promised that the whole earth and its creatures
would never again be destroyed because of the evil that is
lodged in the human heart.

The world that God made remains, although imperfectly.
The secular scientist also lives subject to and in reaction to the
conditions that God created for our existence and to the promises God made to preserve and maintain the earth.

The problem of secular science is not that it is a fiction;
Christian and secular scientists do not live in different worlds.
Rather, having lost their point of orientation secular scientists
account for God's earth in a way that intentionally ignores the
divine role in human events. They have lost the context that
preserves the mystery of existence.

When the ethologist says that the struggle to survive is the
essence of human nature, the Christian need not feel compelled
to counter by claiming that survival is of no consequence at
all. All things being equal, it is probably better to survive than
to succumb; nevertheless, survival is not everything. It is the
relative importance of survival which the secular ethologist
has failed to see.

In a similar fashion, the psychoanalyst overstates the importance of instinctive pleasure, the humanistic psychologist
of self-expression, and the cognitivist of thought. And Christians, supported by the commitments of faith, have the means
for recognizing the value of pleasure, self-expression, and
thought while still maintaining the relativity of all these things.

Thus, they are guarded against the risk of confusing those parts of human experience for the meaning and the mystery of the whole.

What we are talking about perhaps strikes a more familiar note when it is described in other words. We are dealing here with the problem of scientific idolatry. In his writings to the Romans, Paul condemns those who worship the creature instead of the creator; and he is referring to the same ways of unbelief that can corrupt science.

> For although they knew God, they neither glorified him as God nor gave thanks to him, but their thinking became futile and their foolish hearts were darkened. Although they claimed to be wise, they became fools and exchanged the glory of the immortal God for images made to look like mortal man and birds and animals and reptiles (Rom. 1:21–22).

But it is also important to remember that when God condemns idolatry—the worship of wooden and stone idols—it is the unbelief and not the rocks and trees that are condemned. In a parallel fashion, secular science may make an idol of some human function, but it is the distorted account and not the human function itself that is the object of our criticism here.

Where, finally, does this discussion lead us? It cannot address all the problems that the study of emotion raises, but it can provide us with some orientation points. So let us summarize.

1. What we are as persons is defined by the relationship of creature with creator, and this relationship is more fundamental than any other human capacity, action, relationship, or event. At the same time, loving the Lord our God with heart, soul, mind, and strength encompasses the entirety of our lives.

Implicit in our love of God is the desire to fulfill God's purpose for us and to hold in respect all that God made. Thus we are expected to live in harmony with each other and act responsibly toward all God's creatures.

2. Emotions are one dimension of our human constitution through which the deepest meaning of our personhood comes to expression. Our emotions do not define us as persons. However, they do reflect and express our relationship with God and our place in the world.

We express our personhood through those things to which we are responsive and receptive, our inner feelings and intentions, and the tendencies of character and predispositions to action that are formed over a lifetime. Actions of word and deed through which we exercise an influence on others and on the creatures with whom God has placed us in the world also reflect who at heart we are.

3. Emotions are neither good nor bad by nature. When God created us, this capacity was originally good. It expressed the integrity of a perfect humanity in harmony with its creator and at peace with the other creatures.

But through our fall into sin, our emotions were set at odds. Our emotions came to express the tensions of a creation suffering from its resistance to God's harmonious will.

Our emotions like all else about us need to be restored. Only if we are restored and live in the generosity of God's grace can we hope to fully discover what it means to find inner harmony, to live at peace with God's creatures in God's world, and exercise the special responsibility to act on God's behalf as instruments of divine grace.

4. Attempts to conduct scientific inquiry regarding emotion—inquiry outside the bounds of faith—result in distortions of the place and significance of emotion in the lives of persons.

5 Thus, secular theories may be instructive, but they also require our critical interpretation. We can do this best if we weigh them against the knowledge of ourselves that is possible through our believing response to the traditions of Christian faith.